FROM FOOTLIGHTS
TO "THE FLICKERS"

Collectible Sheet Music
Broadway Shows and Silent Movies

MARION SHORT

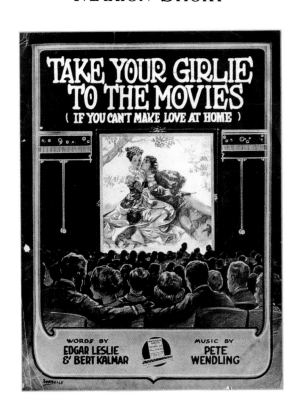

**Photography by
Roy Short**

4880 Lower Valley Road, Atglen, PA 19310 USA

Who'll Take the Place of the Song-Bird Now Gone?
(1923)

In Memoriam—
For the Departed Song-Birds

Joseph Albertson
Cdr. Alvin Brand, USN Ret.
Patricia Cleveland
Edwin Kaplan
Nathaniel Ross

Copyright © 1998 by Marion Short
Library of Congress Catalog Card Number: 97-81428

Designed by Laurie A. Smucker
Typeset in Goudy Sans Lt/Windsor Lt Cn

ISBN: 0-7643-0552-2
Printed in China

Published by Schiffer Publishing Ltd.
4880 Lower Valley Road
Atglen, PA 19310
Phone: (610) 593-1777; Fax: (610) 593-2002
E-mail: schifferbk@aol.com
Please write for a free catalog.
This book may be purchased from the publisher.
Please include $3.95 for shipping.
Try your bookstore first.

We are interested in hearing from authors
with book ideas on related subjects.

Even in its day sheet music was acquired and cherished not only for performance but also for a vague but real "cultural delight." It is easy to disparage a preoccupation with personal property; but it is important, too, to understand that the possession of items of beauty should be seen as serving to elevate the owner, the listener, or the beholder. Historical collections reflect and foster owners who are thereby the more humane, more filled with delight, good taste, and understanding of human history, and thus more responsive to one's fellow citizenry and the democratic society that was part of the collective national vision.

D. W. Krummel
Bibliographical Handbook of American Music
University of Illinois Press, 1988

Acknowledgments

My heartfelt appreciation is extended to all who helped and encouraged me while writing this book. I particularly want to thank James Nelson Brown, Harold Jacobs, and Roy Bishop for the use of examples from their fabulous collections of silent movie music that have added so much to the visual beauty and historical completeness of the book. Thanks to Stan White for most generously providing fine examples of early show business music from his outstanding collection, and for his insightful comments, always so helpful, that pass modestly from his lips. And more thanks to Jennifer Booth and E. J. Hannan for providing music covers for special spots in the book.

Grateful recognition is accorded to all the owners of copyright for the use of examples used to illustrate the historic evolution of show business and silent cinema in America, and to the many legendary performers whose photographs appear on the covers.

My gratitude is further extended to the Schiffer Publishing organization for their faith in the project, and to editor, Dawn Stoltzfus, for her watchful eye in supervising the meshing of text and photographs. And to Roy Short, ever patient and supportive, my continuing thanks for the gargantuan job of photographing the music covers, and for reading the manuscript and catching some of the worst of the errors.

CONTENTS

INTRODUCTION

The two most exciting and stimulating arenas for twentieth century sheet music were the musical comedy stage and the movie theater. The glamour, color, and excitement of musical theater in the United States can be followed in the incredible variety of sheet music from its shows. The moving picture theater from its earliest beginnings was another forum that relied on music to highlight the action on the screen—music that was published for playing and enjoying in one's home after leaving the world of escapism in the darkened theater.

From Footlights to "The Flickers" is divided into two parts; Part One covers show music, and Part Two, silent movie music. Early musical revues, burlesque, vaudeville, and the evolution of shows with a story line are discussed in Part One with appropriate photographs of original song sheet covers illustrating each category.

The chapter that started out as a treatise on "The Big Five" composers of musical comedy show tunes grew into "The Big Five (Or Six, Or Seven)." How can one choose only five from the incredible talents that have written for the stage? My big five grew into six that include Victor Herbert, George M. Cohan, Jerome Kern, Irving Berlin, George Gershwin, and Cole Porter, but this selection of influential composers is a purely personal choice, and I'm certain all will not be in agreement. Some biographical detail is provided for these composers, with special emphasis on their contributions to musical theater, and examples of some of their representative theater songs.

Another chapter examines the changes in musical theater as evidenced by shows since *Show Boat* that emphasize social trends. We have come a long way from the European influenced operettas of the early twentieth century, by tackling subjects as diverse as miscegenation, psychoanalysis, homosexuality, and revolution. Just when one thinks it can't get any better, along comes a production like *Les Miserables* that stirs the emotions and impacts the entire world. Musical theater continues to grow, and owes its popularity to providing timeliness in its artistic presentations.

Silent movies are enjoying a revival, not only at specialty theaters but also on videotape for home viewing. Sheet music with early Hollywood stars on the cover is riding the collectible wave of the future. Part Two with its gallery of silent movie music is my labor of love. The amassing and study of these silent movie theme songs with rare cover photos of early stars holds a special fascination for me, and I like to think my exposition here will help rekindle interest in the early art form of silent movies.

Beginning with Edison's invention of the Vitascope, this book traces the development of the early movie industry and its use of music to enhance the movement on the silent screen, including use of theme songs and cue sheets. Pioneering film-makers who came from New York to Hollywood to break ground in this revolutionary new art form are discussed, and sheet music from their early efforts is shown.

Thumbnail sketches of silent film personalities of yesterday are given along with sheet music examples from their movies. Personal anecdotes about such popular stars as Theda Bara (The Vamp), Mary Pickford (America's Sweetheart), Charlie Chaplin (The Little Tramp), Rudolph Valentino (The Great Lover), and Pearl White (Queen of the Serials) help to add color and nostalgia.

Of particular interest is a chapter on serial photoplays, the chapter movies that were shown at Saturday matinees week after week, keeping audiences coming back to see if their favorite actor or actress survived the terrible peril. Signature theme songs published in conjunction with these serials have photographs of some of the most famous stars of this genre including Pearl White of the famous *Perils of Pauline*.

Indexes are provided enabling the reader to locate a song either by its title or by the show or movie in which it was performed. Price guidelines are included to aid the collector in an intelligent assessment of value, and every effort has been made to give accurate and pertinent information. The author urges you to enjoy this book, and to forgive any grievous errors or omissions.

Opposite page:
There's No Business Like Show Business
With Ethel Merman portraying the raucous gun-toting Annie Oakley, and an inspired score by Irving Berlin, *Annie Get Your Gun* played in New York's Imperial Theater for 1,147 performances. It has had frequent theatrical revivals and was made into a movie in 1950 with Betty Hutton as the colorful "Annie." (1946)

PART ONE

LET'S GO ON WITH THE SHOW!

Musical theater has spawned a wealth of memorable hit songs that are at the top of the list of superior popular music. Songs by master composers like Irving Berlin, George Gershwin, Jerome Kern, and Cole Porter have become true popular classics, enduring through the years. Some sheet music collectors concentrate exclusively on this fruitful and interesting category.

Ideally the collector would like to have a list of all the songs from all the shows, but assembling a list of songs is not as simple as one might think. Sometimes songs were introduced into a show during out-of-town tryouts, and then were later dropped. In other instances songs were issued as professional copies, marked as such with plain unillustrated covers, then were not used in the show and were never actually published commercially. Frequently songs were not a part of the original score, but were interpolated into a long running show to attract audiences. The collector must decide just how complete a collection he wants, and go from there.

A collection of show tunes can be effectively organized by sorting the shows alphabetically into two groups—large size from 1900 to 1919, and standard size from 1920 to the present. With this type of organization the shows are easy to locate. It should be noted that sheet music covers from a particular show are generally all alike, and only the songs inside are different—an early merchandising ploy to publicize the show itself.

CHAPTER 1:
MUSICAL SHOWS WITH A PLOT

Musical productions in the United States during the Gay Nineties included burlesques, extravaganzas, farce comedies, and comic operas—genres that were all stepping stones to modern musical comedy theater. Musical theater was developing along two main streams, not always mutually exclusive, eventually dichotomizing into either musical plays with a plot or shows that were more of a variety revue. Certain landmark productions mark the development of musical shows with a plot.

One of the first musical plays in the United States was *The Black Crook* (1866), an extravaganza with a story line, music, and dance. Critics in some quarters described it as an "indecent and demoralizing exhibition" because of its ballet by one hundred voluptuous French dancers in flesh-colored tights, but such criticism only served to lure in a curious public who filled the theater to capacity for sixteen months. The plot was inconsequential, merely a skeleton on which to display five hours' worth of dancing girls, colorful costumes and scenery, and many other changing attractions, but *The Black Crook* was still an unprecedented success, running in New York for a respectable 474 performances, the longest run up to that time of any play. Its popularity continued unsurpassed for more than 25 years, with eight revivals in New York and road tours to such distant hinterlands as Provo, Utah.

Evangeline (1874) was a burlesque of the Henry Wadsworth Longfellow epic poem with an original score by **Edward E. Rice** and lyrics by **J. Cheever Goodwin**. It was less dependent on the European traditions of French ballet

I Think So, Don't You?
Miss Annie Boyd appears on the cover of a song from *Evangeline*, dressed in a revealing costume that caused raised eyebrows in some circles, but didn't deter audiences from flocking to see the show. (1888 printing) *Collection of Stan White*

Black Crook Pas de Demons
The Black Crook was a musical extravaganza first presented at Niblo's Gardens in New York in 1866. It is generally recognized as the first true musical comedy in America. This ballet music, composed by W.D.C. Botefuhr, was used in a revival performance at the Varieties Theater in St. Louis. (ca. 1866) *Collection of Stan White*

and German melodrama than its predecessor, *The Black Crook*. Aware of the allure of feminine pulchritude, Rice also clothed many of his girls in tights, including young Fay Templeton, the prima donna who played the leading male role of Gabriel. Rice described this venture as a musical comedy, the first time the term was used in connection with American musical theater. *Evangeline* was well-received, and helped to pave the way for future musical productions with a story line.

The popular extravaganza *Adonis* (1884) was a burlesque of the story of Pygmalion and Galatea starring the matinee idol Henry E. Dixey, a singer and dancer who was a favorite with the ladies. The basic plot revolved around the adventures of a statue that came to life, and situations and songs were frequently changed to keep audiences coming back. It played a record 603 performances at the Bijou Opera House in New York.

Edward Harrigan and **Tony Hart** wrote a series of Mulligan Guard farce-comedies between 1877 and 1885 that used familiar Bowery locales and characters. Though they were straight plays, Harrigan and Hart interpolated catchy songs by staff composer David Braham that soon became popular around town. To the popular *Mulligan Guard* series, they added the *Skidmore Guard* based on a comic group of black militiamen, and many "Skidmore" related songs were presented. A theater fire in 1884 destroyed many of the scores and parts of Braham's music, but published sheet music can still be found of some of the interpolated songs.

A Trip To Chinatown, mounted by Charles Hoyt in 1890, was a farce-comedy set in big-city San Francisco. It too had a plot of sorts, but emphasis was more on musical acts and comedy routines. Though Hoyt's humor was criticized in the *Boston Transcript* as smacking more of the barroom than the drawing room, the show toured the United States for a year, then settled in at the Madison Square Theatre in New York for a lengthy run of 650 performances. The show was modernized and renamed *A Winsome Widow* by Florenz Ziegfeld in 1912. He used some of his *Follies'* regulars, Leon Errol, the Dolly Sisters, and Mae West as the baby vamp, La Petite Daffy, in some of the performances.

Talamea Waltz Song
Lillian Grubb starred in the original production of Edward Rice and Henry Dixey's *Adonis* singing this waltz song written especially for her. (1886 printing) *Collection of Stan White*

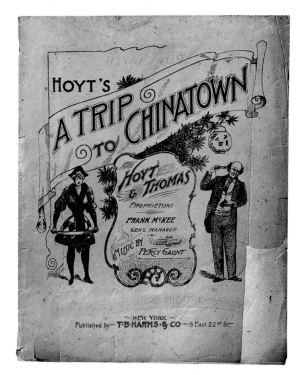

A Trip to Chinatown Song Book
Much of the popularity of Charles Hoyt's comedy *A Trip to Chinatown* was attributed to the original score by Percy Gaunt. "The Bowery," a popular song from the show, sold several hundred thousand copies. Not only did the song immortalize the Bowery section of New York, but it also proved to early publishers how lucrative it was to publish popular Broadway show tunes. (1892)

The comic operas hailing from Europe were a far cry from the farce-comedies of America's Harrigan and Hart. Comic opera was introduced in the United States in 1878 with the delightful *H.M.S. Pinafore* by the English team of **Sir William S. Gilbert** (1836-1911) and **Sir Arthur Sullivan** (1842-1900) followed by such offerings as *The Pirates of Penzance* (1879) and *The Mikado* (1885). They became the style-setters for operettas relying on a good plot for continuity, and using songs as part of the play. Composers Victor Herbert, Sigmund Romberg, and Rudolf Friml carried on this form in their light operettas.

Other well-trained and cultivated authors and composers found their way to the New York stage from Europe. Viennese composer **Franz Lehár's** (1870-1948) influence was felt with the introduction of his operetta *The Merry Widow* in 1907. The "Merry Widow Waltz" closed the second act, and the audience clamored for encores. The show ran for a year in New York, and ladies from the audience were soon wearing Merry Widow hats and dresses, and dancing to the lilting strains of the popular title waltz.

The Melody of Love
The Franz Lehár operetta *Gypsy Love* was coolly received by audiences who found it too operatic and heavy. It ran for only 31 performances. (1911)

Ivan Caryll (1861-1921) was a distinguished Belgian composer with many European successes. He started as musical director of the Gaiety Theatre in London in 1891, and became an influential figure in British musical comedy, writing many popular shows. Caryll's reputation preceded him when he came to America in 1911, and he continued his string of successes in New York with *The Pink Lady* which played to capacity crowds at the New Amsterdam Theatre

Merry Widow Waltz
Franz Lehár's lovely waltz from his 1907 operetta enjoyed new popularity when presented in the Metro-Goldwyn-Mayer film *The Merry Widow* starring Jeanette MacDonald and Maurice Chevalier. (1934)

My Beautiful Lady
Audiences for *The Pink Lady* were entranced by lovely Hazel Dawn, dressed all in pink, as she played Ivan Caryll's "Beautiful Lady" on her violin, starting a fad for that color in ladies' fashions. (1911)

11

Oskar Straus (1870-1954) brought over his comic opera *A Waltz Dream* from Vienna to New York in 1908 giving *The Merry Widow* some healthy competition. The following year he introduced *The Chocolate Soldier*, adapted by Stanislaus Stange from George Bernard Shaw's comedy *Arms and the Man*, and it had a successful run of 296 performances.

for 320 performances before going on a successful cross-country tour. Drama critics praised it for its amusing book and pleasing music, insisting that everyone should see *The Pink Lady* to discover what a musical comedy should be. Other Caryll successes include *Oh! Oh! Delphine* (1912), *The Belle of Bond Street* (1914), *Jack O'Lantern* (1917), and *The Girl Behind the Gun* (1918).

My Hero
This waltz by Oscar Straus with words by Stanislaus Stange was the major hit song of *The Chocolate Soldier*. Sheet music has a colorful cover drawing by Andre De Takacs of the soldier with a young maiden. (1909)

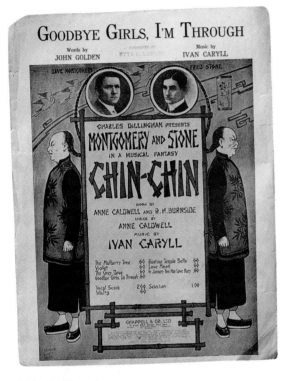

Goodbye Girls, I'm Through
Chin-Chin was described as an oriental musical fantasy, and the two stars, Dave Montgomery and Fred Stone, were dressed in coolie costumes with long pigtails. The show was an immediate success and ran for 295 performances at the Globe Theatre before it toured the country. This Ivan Caryll hit song was performed by Fred Stone. (1914)

Show Songs of Hoschna and Hauerbach

Karl Hoschna (1877-1911) studied piano, harmony, and composition at the Vienna Conservatory, and played oboe in Victor Herbert's band before composing operettas. His first big success was the score for *Three Twins*, adapted from a farce written by the wife of California's Governor Pacheco, with lyrics by **Otto Hauerbach** (1873-1963)—a felicitous combination. Hauerbach was an English teacher and newspaper reporter before turning his writing skills to librettos and lyrics. Successful collaborations by Hauerbach and Hoschna in 1910 were *Katy Did*, *Madame Sherry*, *The Girl of My Dreams*, and *Bright Eyes*. Hoschna's untimely death a little over a year after the premiere of *Madame Sherry* put an end to his career at the height of his powers. Hauerbach (now respelled Harbach) went on to a successful collaboration with composers Rudolph Friml, Vincent Youmans, George Gershwin, Jerome Kern, and Sigmund Romberg.

Good Night Sweetheart, Goodnight
This is one of two different song covers used for the production *Three Twins*, the first theatrical success of Karl Hoschna and Otto Hauerbach. (1908)

Doctor Tinkle Tinker
Cover star Leila McIntyre shared billing with John Hyams in this Hauerbach/Hoschna collaboration for the show *The Girl of My Dreams*. The two are shown in the lower left photo. (1910)

Cuddle Up a Little Closer
Though Karl Hoschna wrote this song for a vaudeville sketch some years prior to the show's production, it wasn't until Bessie McCoy sang it in *Three Twins* that it became a hit. (1908)

Every Little Movement
Little Lina Abarbanell, fresh from her success in *The Merry Widow*, dazzled audiences with her rendition of this famous song from *Madame Sherry* composed by Hoschna with suggestive lyrics by Hauerbach, "Every little movement has a meaning all its own." (1910)

Rudolf Friml Show Songs

Rudolf Friml (1879-1972) was a classically trained Czech musician who studied with eminent composer Dvorák in Prague. A composer and concert pianist, Friml came to the United States in the early 1900s on a concert tour accompanying the virtuoso violinist Jan Kubelik. He wrote many piano, violin, and cello compositions, and performed his own piano concerto with the New York Symphony in Carnegie Hall. He met with greater success in the musical comedy field with his first operetta score written for *The Firefly* in 1912. He abandoned his concert career, and became one of the great operetta composers of the 1920s, credited with 27 musical comedies including *High Jinks* (1914), *Katinka* (1915), *Rose Marie* (1924), *The Vagabond King* (1925), and *The Three Musketeers* (1928).

Ev'ry Little While
The Three Musketeers starred Dennis King as D'Artagnan in a sumptuous production by Florenz Ziegfeld of the Alexandre Dumas swashbuckler tale. With music by Rudolph Friml, lyrics by P. G. Wodehouse and Clifford Grey, sets by Joseph Urban, and elaborate period costumes by John Harkrider, the show was a critical success, and had a healthy run. (1928)

Something Seems Tingle-Ingleing
Rudolf Friml's stage hit *High Jinks* followed the success of *The Firefly*. It was a lighthearted musical farce about a magical perfume, and featured this lilting catchy tune with words by Otto Hauerbach. High Jinks was the name of the perfume, and in a promotional stunt of questionable taste, samples were sprayed on unsuspecting theatergoers at every performance. (1913)

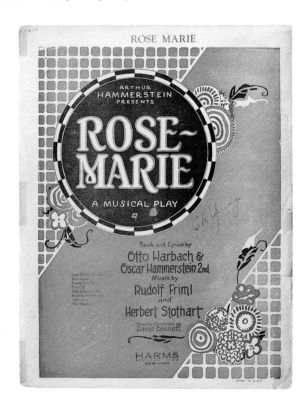

Rose Marie
Friml's operetta *Rose Marie* was one of the major musical events of 1924, eventually playing 557 performances. The original cast included Dennis King and Mary Ellis and the colorful presence of the Canadian Royal Mounted Police involved in a manhunt. (1924)

Sigmund Romberg Show Songs

Sigmund Romberg (1887-1951) was a skilled composer from Hungary who worked for four years on staff at the Winter Garden writing for the *Passing Show* and other revues. His first successful musical comedy was *Follow Me* in 1916 starring popular Anna Held flashing her come-hither eyes and singing "I Want to be Good but My Eyes Won't Let Me." Romberg's lengthy career included more than fifty musicals, many of which were successful operettas in the Viennese tradition. Many of his most memorable songs are from the scores of *The Student Prince* (1924), *The Desert Song* (1926), and *The New Moon* (1927). Romberg also wrote scores for Hollywood films in the 1930s, and toured the country with his own concert orchestra.

Song of the Vagabonds
Dennis King portrayed the swashbuckling hero, Francois Villon, in this long-running musical *The Vagabond King* based on the drama *If I Were King* by Justin Huntley McCarthy. This stirring song by Rudolf Friml arranged for male voices, plus the lyrical "Only a Rose" were two of the hits from the operetta. (1925)

Gather the Rose
The White Eagle was based on the famous and popular play *The Squaw Man* by Edwin Milton Royle. Despite Friml's fine music with the book and lyrics by Brian Hooker and W. H. Post, it failed at the box-office. It's not surprising, considering the competition that year included *Show Boat*, *Hit the Deck*, *Good News*, *Rio Rita*, and *A Connecticut Yankee*. (1928)

Go Away, Girls
Composed by Romberg with lyrics by Rida Johnson Young, the Messrs. Shubert production of *Maytime* is described on the song cover as a play with music. The waltz "Will You Remember" was the biggest hit of the show, with its recurring theme played throughout. Cover art designed by Raeburn Van Buren. (1917)

15

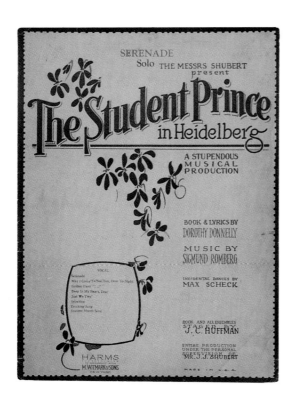

Serenade
The Student Prince, considered by many to contain Romberg's finest score, ran for 608 performances, the most for any Romberg show. Other fine songs from the play were "Deep in My Heart, Dear," "Just We Two," and the lively "Drinking Song." (1925)

The Riff Song
This was one of Romberg's best songs from *The Desert Song*, sung by the Riff's dashing leader, The Red Shadow. Other memorable songs were "The Desert Song" and "One Alone." (1926)

I Dare Not Love You
Romberg's contribution to light opera in 1925 was *Princess Flavia*, a musical version of Anthony Hope's *Prisoner of Zenda*, with book and lyrics by Harry B. Smith. (1925)

Lover, Come Back to Me
Romberg's score for *The New Moon* contains many excellent songs that have retained their place in the light opera repertoire. Familiar tunes are "One Kiss," "Softly, As in a Morning Sunrise," "Stouthearted Men," and "Wanting You." (1927)

Show Songs by Howard, Hough, and Adams

Chicago was another hub of theatrical activity. **Will M. Hough, Frank R. Adams,** and **Joseph E. Howard** collaborated on several musical shows from about 1905 to 1915, with Hough and Adams writing the book and lyrics and Howard composing the music. A lot of sheet music is around from the shows of this prolific team, including songs from *The Time, the Place, and the Girl* (1907), *Honeymoon Trail* (1908), *The Goddess of Liberty* (1909), *The Sweetest Girl in Paris* (1910), *A Broadway Honeymoon* (1911), *Love and Politics* (1911), *Lower Berth Thirteen* (1912), and *In and Out* (1915). Sheet music covers from these shows are distinguished by their vivid colors and fanciful artwork, many of them designed by Starmer.

Right:
The Land of Used-to-Be
Hough, Adams, and Howard collaborated on this musical comedy *The Golden Girl* presented by Mort H. Singer at the La Salle Theatre in Chicago. Starmer cover. (1909)

Just Say You Care
Joe Howard wrote both the book and music for *The Flower of the Ranch*, a western play produced by the Askin-Singer Company starring Mabel Barrison. Vivid cover art was created by Starmer. (1907)

I Wonder Who's Kissing Her Now
This well-known song from *The Prince of To-night* has enjoyed several revivals and sold millions of copies of sheet music through the years. Joe Howard's authorship of the song was later disputed by Harold Orlob, one of Howard's staff composers, who successfully sued for recognition as the sole composer of the song. This original edition shows a handsome prince dressed in white and gold, smoking a cigarette in a moonlit forest. (1909)

The Dear Little Ghost of Your Smile
The prolific team of Hough, Adams, and Howard wrote *Miss Nobody from Starland*, another Mort Singer production, staged at the Princess Theatre in Chicago. Cover art of a beautiful lady in a luxurious feathered chapeau was created by Starmer. (1910)

Jack O'Lantern
The Flirting Princess ran at Chicago's La Salle Theatre. The song covers not only credit the three songwriters, Hough, Adams, and Howard, but also give credit for the special musical numbers composed by Harold Orlob that are included in the list of songs from the show. (1909)

Besides delineating fashion, song covers from musical shows contain a wealth of information about the shows, producers, stars, composers and lyricists, and the theaters of the day. The gargantuan Hippodrome theater cost $1,750,000 to build, and was completed in 1905. It was a huge edifice with a stage 110 feet deep and 200 feet wide, and contained more than 5,000 seats, with a dressing room section that accommodated another 1,000. The stage apron could hold two regulation-size circus rings, and under the apron was a deep tank filled with water for use in aquatic sequences. The theater was the setting for many spectacular extravaganzas through the years.

Poor Butterfly
The popular Puccini opera *Madame Butterfly* served as the inspiration for this song by John Golden and Raymond Hubbell that became an enormous hit. It was first performed in *The Big Show* at the Hippodrome by an Oriental vaudevillian who was soon replaced by Sophie Bernard who sang it to success. Cover art by Burton Rice. (1916)

Cheer Up, Liza
The second act of *Cheer Up* caused a sensation when a full-size freight train chugged across the mammoth stage at the Hippodrome. Cover by Burton Rice. (1917)

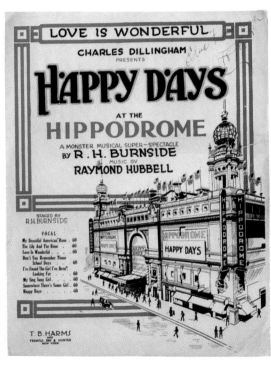

Love Is Wonderful
A wonderful drawing of New York's legendary Hippodrome appears on song covers from the show *Happy Days*, described as "a monster musical super-spectacle." (1919)

Composer **Will Marion Cook** and poet **Paul Laurence Dunbar** came into prominence in 1898 with their musical comedy *Clorindy, the Origin of the Cakewalk*. Cakewalk dancing and a twenty-six voice African-American chorus enlivened the rousing finale of "Darktown Is Out Tonight," inspiring a standing ovation on opening night. Other successful shows by Cook followed—*In Dahomey* (1902), *In Abyssinia* (1906), and *In Bandana Land* (1907). Talented black songwriters like **Bob Cole** and the **Johnson Brothers** also made substantial contributions to early twentieth century musicals.

Come Out Dinah on the Green
Bob Cole and J. W. Johnson wrote the lyrics to Rosamond Johnson's music in this popular song from the Klaw and Erlanger production of the extravaganza *The Sleeping Beauty and the Beast*. (1901)

The charismatic young American composer George M. Cohan tackled American musical theater in a different way, avoiding the farcical clichés that Hoyt used in *A Trip to Chinatown*. Cohan's plots had a new freshness, revolving around ordinary American people with whom the audience could identify. Popular songs, dances, ensemble pieces, and spoken dialogue were all related to the plot. But it took the genius of Jerome Kern in the 1920s to develop a truly Americanized musical comedy form which incorporated both popular music and operetta, yet was not as primitive as the feisty Cohan productions. Kern was able to transfer the romance and sentimentality of the European operetta style to a style that could be embraced by ordinary people, a musical comedy style uniquely American with a strong story line.

A Gallery of Early 20th Century Broadway Show Songs

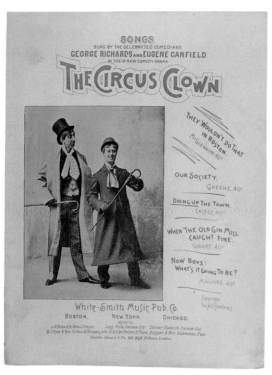

Doing Up the Town
This rollicking drinking song by Harry Castle was a popular favorite as performed by celebrated comedians George Richards and Eugene Canfield in the comedy drama *The Circus Clown*. (1894)

Yip-I-Addy-I-Ay
This outstanding song by Will Cobb and John Flynn was written for the relatively obscure Joe Weber satire *The Merry Widow and the Devil*. It's a rollicking waltz that became a specialty of singer Blanche Ring who reportedly sang it with great verve and passion. (1908)

Sammy
Fairy-tales and fantasy continued as vehicles for musical comedy with the season's major hit *The Wizard of Oz*, an adaptation of L. Frank Baum's novel. Cover star Grace Kimball interpolated this song into the production, but was soon replaced by Lotta Faust. (1902)

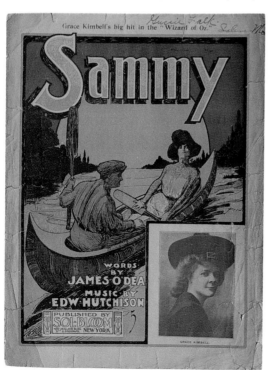

Has Anybody Here Seen Kelly?
Nora Bayes made a hit out of this lively song about an Irishman named Kelly, an interpolated song in *The Jolly Bachelors*, a Lew Fields' production. The song was an English import, but it didn't become popular in the United States until William McKenna wrote this Americanized version. (1909)

Take Plenty of Shoes
Many show covers featured photographs of female stars wearing fashions of the day. Entertainer Marie Cahill in *The Boys and Betty* wore a big feathered hat of the period, and a dress made of lavish ribbon embroidery over net. For a further touch of elegance she carries a luxurious fur muff. (1908)

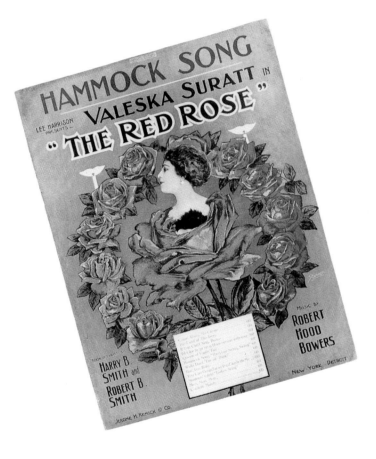

Hammock Song
Valeska Suratt designed her own flamboyant costumes for *The Red Rose*, including a flaming rainbow-hued harem skirt, and a gaudy Spanish inspired outfit in canary yellow and black. In keeping with the musical's theme, the entire cast wore red roses, and red roses were given away at the door on opening night. (1911)

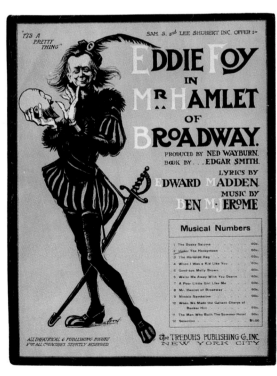

Under the Honeymoon
Eddie Foy was a popular personality in vaudeville, a dancer and comedian who subsequently appeared in many Broadway musicals. Cover caricature of Foy was drawn by artist John Frew for the show songs from *Mr. Hamlet of Broadway*. (1908)

The Fascinating Widow
Female impersonator Julian Eltinge, a classy cross-dresser in his own right, good-naturedly imitated Valeska Suratt in this play about life in a college girls' dormitory. Eltinge was described as charming and well-groomed, and had many fans during a long and successful career. (1910)

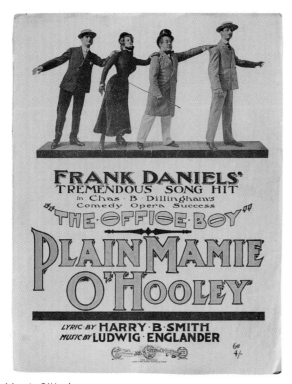

Plain Mamie O'Hooley
Austrian-born Ludwig Englander was a popular composer of musical comedies in the early years of the twentieth century. This song, with lyrics by Harry B. Smith, was written for Frank Daniels in the comic opera *The Office Boy*. (1903)

Tillie's Nightmare
Marie Dressler (1869-1934), star of *Tillie's Nightmare*, is better known today for her movie work in *Tugboat Annie* and *Min and Bill*, for which she won Best Actress Academy Award in 1930-31. She was a Broadway star long before her incursion into films, both in vaudeville and the legitimate stage. She entered movies in 1914 co-starring with Charlie Chaplin in Hollywood's version of *Tillie's Nightmare*. Her biggest song hit in this Lew Fields' show was "Heaven Will Protect the Working Girl." (1909)

Opposite page:
They're All Sweeties
Lovely ladies from the *Follies* appear on cover with Billy Glason who introduced this song written by Andrew Sterling and Harry Von Tilzer. (1919)

CHAPTER 2:
THE MUSICAL REVUE

Burlesque of the earthier "girlie" type appeared on the scene in 1868 when Lydia Thompson and her statuesque British Blondes invaded New York with the musical *Ixion, or the Man at the Wheel*, another of the infamous shows with girls in tights—again shocking and titillating the American public. This exhibitionism paved the way for later musical extravaganzas which emphasized feminine beauty and pulchritude in lavish, though revealing, costumes. The Gaiety Girls from London appeared in 1894, replaced in 1900 by the six beauteous native-born Florodora Girls, followed later by the Ziegfeld Follies Girls, and the Nell Brinkley Bathing Beauties. Musical revues continued to evolve from the girlie type of show introduced by Lydia Thompson's high-kicking showgirls to an olio of loosely strung together variety acts. They often had a single unifying theme rather than a story plot, carrying on the minstrel show and vaudeville traditions.

The English import *Florodora* had a successful run in New York due in part to the well-publicized six Florodora Girls, advertised as the most beautiful women on the stage. Their beguiling sextette in the second act was a winner, and helped to make the show a success. Their partners, the six Gentle Strangers sang "Tell me, Pretty Maiden, are there any more at home like you?", to which the dainty maidens coyly responded, "There are a few," all the while smiling and winking at the men. The Florodora Girls were frequently replaced, as many succumbed to the entreaties of their admirers, and retired to marry wealthy men.

Tell Me Pretty Maiden
Florodora was an import from the London stage where it ran for 400 performances. It opened in New York in 1900, and became a huge long-running hit with 505 performances, largely due to the charm and beauty of the six *Florodora* girls who beguiled audiences with their rendition of this song. (1901)

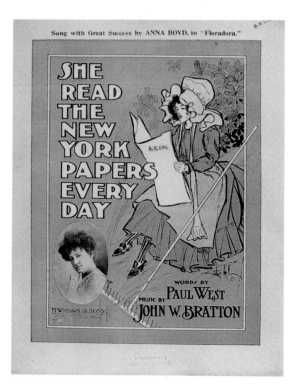

She Read the New York Papers Every Day
A show of *Florodora's* longevity benefited from insertion of new material. Anna Boyd interpolated this song by Paul West and John Bratton in an early production. Cover art by Edgar Keller. *Collection of Stan White*

Minstrel troupes reached the New York stage in the mid-nineteenth century with a unique type of musical revue. With roots in the African-American tradition, it enjoyed quite a heyday despite its low-brow humor. Minstrel shows were the staging areas for some excellent songs by esteemed songwriters James Bland and Stephen Foster, and for the syncopated idioms of ragtime.

The Island of Roses and Love
Elegant Miss Lillian Russell added a touch of class to the Weber and Fields musical *Jubilee*, seen here on the cover of a song hit by Earle Jones and Neil Moret. Cover by Starmer. (1911)

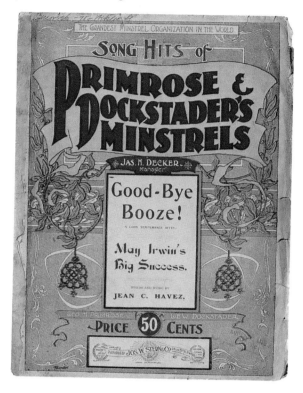

Good-Bye Booze!
This comic song about the evils of drink was one of May Irwin's big successes in the Lew Dockstader and George Primrose Minstrel show. Cover design by Starmer. (1901)

Comedians Joe Weber and Lew Fields branched out into production with their Weber and Fields Music Hall revues that started in 1895 and lasted until 1904. Using comedy sketches and burlesque travesties of current plays, headline stars like Lillian Russell and Fay Templeton, and musical production numbers with lots of beautiful girls, they managed to eliminate the more prurient aspects of earlier burlesque, and continued to forge the way for the later more sophisticated variety shows.

Minstrel shows were eventually outmoded by variety shows like those offered by theatrical entrepreneur Tony Pastor at his Music Hall. In 1865 Pastor left his career as a circus clown and went into show business in New York presenting wholesome vaudeville shows the whole family could enjoy, and appealing to women by offering free dress patterns and sewing kits. He was soon doing standing room only business. His stage became an audition arena for budding talent. Many a future star would start out under Pastor's aegis, including Helen Louise Leonard who changed her name to the more euphonious sounding Lillian Russell.

Miss Russell reached stardom in the 1885 Rice production *Polly, the Pet of the Regiment*, and went on to become the darling of American musical theater starring in many Weber and Fields burlesques. Sumptuous gowns that she designed herself displayed her hourglass figure, and her clear well-trained lyric soprano voice and renowned beauty kept her at the forefront of popular appeal.

My Blushin' Rosie
Fay Templeton starred in many Weber and Fields shows, singing this piece with words by Edgar Smith and music by John Stromberg in their production *Fiddle-Dee-Dee*. (1910)

When Reuben Comes to Town
The Rogers Brothers, Gus and Max, produced a series of successful vaudeville farces patterned after the Weber and Fields Dutch-humored shows, and enjoyed a modicum of popularity until Gus Rogers died in 1908. Cover photo shows the brothers and their partners in vaudeville attire for the show *In Central Park*. (1900)

Ziegfeld Follies

A Pretty Girl Is like a Melody [movie: *The Great Ziegfeld*]
Florenz Ziegfeld, the famous Broadway producer of the renowned *Ziegfeld Follies*, was known as the great glorifier of the American girl. He was portrayed by Walter Pidgeon in the Metro-Goldwyn-Mayer biographical production of *The Great Ziegfeld*. (1936)

A Pretty Girl Is Like a Melody
Ziegfeld needed a "staircase song" for his *Ziegfeld Follies of 1919*, and Irving Berlin obliged with this song he considered one of his best. It was sung in the show by John Steel as a parade of statuesque Ziegfeld beauties descended an ornate staircase. (1919)

In 1896 a young showman of daring and imagination appeared on the Broadway scene, and changed the history of musical theater. Florenz Ziegfeld (1867-1932) had a background in theater through the strong influence of his father who founded the Chicago Musical College. His early experience included managing Eugene Sandow, a famous strong man, at the Chicago World's Fair of 1893, and work with Lew Weber of Weber and Fields on a show at the Music Hall. But he had far grander dreams that came to fruition when he went to Europe and discovered the piquant and pretty singer Anna Held. He placed her under contract and brought her to New York to star in his musical shows.

Was There Ever a Pal Like You
Billie Burke was a stage actress in England before coming to Broadway where she soon became the toast of the town, eventually becoming Ziegfeld's second wife. She carried on the Ziegfeld show tradition after his death to help pay off his gambling debts. Her delicate coloring and soft loveliness are captured on this pastel lithograph cover by W. F. Powers Company. (1919)

Follow Me Around
After Anna Held was divorced from Florenz Ziegfeld, she continued her successful stage career. Still lovely and retaining her astonishing small-waisted figure, she starred in the musical comedy *Follow Me*, singing one of her numbers dressed in milk-white tights. Anna Held died two years later from a combination of rigorous dieting and over-zealous lacing of her waist. (1917)

I Just Can't Make My Eyes Behave
Miss Anna Held, flashing her famous seductive eyes, appears on the cover of a popular song written by Will Cobb and Gus Edwards for the Ziegfeld production *A Parisian Model*. So successful was her rendition that she took it as her theme song thereafter.(1906)

Anna Held (1873-1918) made her American debut in *A Parlor Match* at the Herald Square Theatre in New York in 1896. Her big song from the show was the coquettish "Won't You Come and Play With Me?" Other hit shows followed—*La Poupee* (1897), *Papa's Wife* (1899), *The Little Duchess* (1901), *Mam'selle Napoleon* (1903), *Higgledy Piggledy* (1904), *A Parisian Model* (1906), and *Miss Innocence* (1908). Anna Held was at the peak of her popularity when Florenz Ziegfeld featured her in his first *Follies* show.

Ziegfeld's *Follies of 1907* was patterned after the famous Folies Bergère of Paris, a show that Ziegfeld found most enchanting on his European trips. This modest production that cost only $13,000 featured Nora Bayes, Grace La Rue, Helen Broderick, and Anna Held with fifty beautiful girls. It started a tradition that was repeated successfully for more than twenty years. Ziegfeld was married to Anna Held for several years, and after their divorce in 1913 he married the actress Billie Burke.

Hold Me In Your Loving Arms
This song with lyrics by Gene Buck and music by Louis Hirsch was introduced in the scintillating *Ziegfeld Follies of 1915*. Bubbly zestful cover art was created by Andre De Takacs. (1915)

I've Saved All My Love for You
Some of Broadway's most legendary stars appeared in *Ziegfeld Follies of 1916*—Will Rogers, W. C. Fields, Fannie Brice, Bert Williams, and Marion Davies. It ran for 112 performances. (1916)

Luana Lou
Ziegfeld's Midnight Frolic was a lavish night club show presented on the New Amsterdam Theatre Roof where patrons could drink, dine, and dance in a relaxed cabaret atmosphere after the regular *Follies* evening show. The *Frolics* series ran between 1915 and 1921 and was a profitable Ziegfeld venture. Ziegfeld chorines in exotic hula outfits highlighted this production number. (1916)

Syncopated Tune
This lavish production of *Ziegfeld Follies 1918* introduced talented Marilyn Miller to *Follies'* audiences, along with Ziegfeld's other line-up of stars—this time, Eddie Cantor, W. C. Fields, Lillian Lorraine, Will Rogers, Joe Frisco, and the gorgeous ladies of the *Follies*. (1918)

My Baby's Arms
Ziegfeld Follies 1919 was the most popular *Follies* ever. Besides its lovely women and fabulous costumes and sets, it featured many stars including Eddie Cantor, Eddie Dowling, Marilyn Miller, Van and Schenck, and Bert Williams. Other notable songs were several by Irving Berlin including "A Pretty Girl Is Like a Melody," "You'd Be Surprised," and "Mandy." (1919)

Your Sunny Southern Smile
Ziegfeld always used the best talent around to publicize his *Follies*. He discovered artist Alberto Vargas long before Vargas became famous for his *Esquire* magazine centerfolds, and employed him from 1919 to 1931 to paint watercolor portraits of the beautiful *Follies'* showgirls for display in the theater lobby. Several Vargas paintings were also used on sheet music covers. (1931)

You Can Make My Life a Bed of Roses
Ziegfeld had trouble raising money for his musical comedy *Hot-Cha*, and had to ask notorious mobsters Dutch Schultz and Waxey Gordon to back it. He had enough talent lined up to put it over—songs by Lew Brown and Ray Henderson, dancing by Eleanor Powell and the team of Velez and Yolanda, and the comedy of Bert Lahr who bumbles his way into bullfighting in Mexico—but the show folded in June 1932 after a short run. Ziegfeld died a month later. (1932)

31

Show Girl Sweeties
from the *Ziegfeld Follies*

Bring Back My Blushing Rose (front cover)
Ziegfeld showgirls frame this song cover from *Ziegfeld Follies 1921*.
The music was written by distinguished composer Rudolf Friml, with
words by Gene Buck.

Hold Me (front cover)
Ziegfeld beauties fill the front cover of this song sheet from *Ziegfeld
Follies 1920*.

Hold Me (back cover)
More Ziegfeld lovelies adorn the back cover from *Ziegfeld Follies 1920*.

Bring Back My Blushing Rose (back cover)
Ziegfeld showgirls are garbed in sumptuous costumes and exotic
chapeaux created by costume and set designer James Reynolds for
Ziegfeld Follies 1921.

List'ning on Some Radio (front cover)
Beautiful girls on song covers apparently sell a lot of sheet music.
Ziegfeld chorines are again featured on the front cover of a popular
song from the 16th edition *Ziegfeld Follies 1922*.

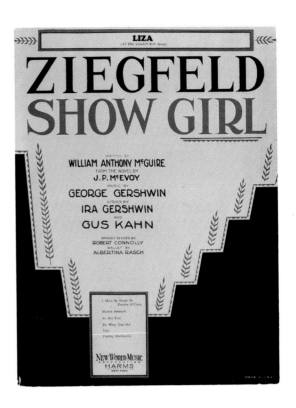

Liza
This song written by George and Ira Gershwin for *Ziegfeld Show Girl*
was performed by Ruby Keeler descending a staircase adorned with
one hundred statuesque showgirls. She was sometimes helped by her
husband, Al Jolson, who tried to assuage her stage fright by leaping
from his seat in the audience to sing a second chorus. (1929)

List'ning on Some Radio (back cover)
Another bevy of Ziegfeld beauties from *Ziegfeld Follies 1922* are
splashed across the back cover.

If I Can't Get the Sweetie I Want
Evelyn Law starred in several Ziegfeld shows of the 1920s. She was a
pretty little high-kicking dancer, and amazed audiences with her
ability to forward kick to ten inches over her head. (1923)

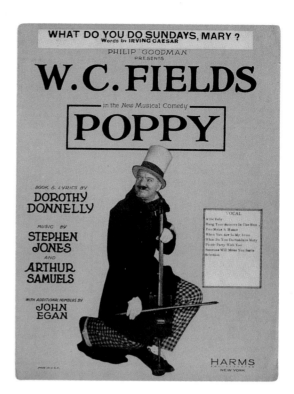

You're a Great Big Lonesome Baby
Marion Davies was a beautiful blonde dancer in Ziegfeld's 1916 *Follies* when she was discovered by newspaper tycoon William Randolph Hearst, who fell madly in love with her and took charge of her career. The following year she left the Ziegfeld company to make her first Hollywood movie, *Runaway Romany*. (1917)

What Do You Do Sundays, Mary?
W. C. Fields was a vaudeville headliner act when Ziegfeld aide, Gene Buck, collared him for the 1915 *Follies*. Fields' wry deadpan comedy style was popular with audiences, and he performed in every *Follies* from 1915 through 1921, writing many of his own hilarious scripts. This cover photo shows him playing the lead in the hit show *Poppy* after he left the *Follies*. (1923) *Collection of Harold Jacobs*

Other *Ziegfeld* Stars

My Isle of Golden Dreams
The glamorous Dolly Sisters were thought by many to be twins, but there were ten years difference in their ages. They danced in Ziegfeld's 1911 *Follies*, his show *A Winsome Widow*, and some early editions of the *Midnight Frolic*. They are seen on cover of a song from the 1918 show *Oh, Look!*

You Can't Keep a Good Girl Down
Ziegfeld starred Marilyn Miller in the title role of *Sally*, aided by the comic antics of *Follies'* regular, Leon Errol. Errol was a *Follies'* cast member from 1911 through 1915, and also directed some of the Ziegfeld shows. Song covers for *Sally* were published in a two color version and this more sought after full color version. (1920) *Collection of Harold Jacobs*

The Moon Shines on the Moonshine
Bert Williams was one of the top comics in the *Follies*, and was a regular in eight editions between 1910 and 1919. When Prohibition reared its ugly head in 1919, this comic song about making booze in a still was a specialty of Williams that was enjoyed by a thirsty public. (1920)

Second Hand Rose
This song by Grant Clarke and James F. Hanley was another big hit for Fannie Brice in the *Ziegfeld Follies of 1921*. It became familiar to another generation when sung by Barbra Streisand in the award winning 1968 film *Funny Girl* based on the life of Fannie Brice. The striking Art Deco cover was designed by Wohlman. (1921)

My Man
Fannie Brice, one of Ziegfeld's greatest stars, surprised her public who expected humor from her by singing the tragic song "My Man (Mon Homme)" with such deep emotion that it moved the audience to tears. Her rendition was the big hit of the *Follies of 1921*.

All She'd Say Was Umh-Hum
August van Glone and Joe Schenck were better known as Van and Schenck in *Ziegfeld's Follies*. They started out in vaudeville, and were picked up by Ziegfeld in 1916 to perform their entertaining singing act in his shows. They were with Ziegfeld for several years and appear on many sheet music covers of *Follies'* songs. (1920)

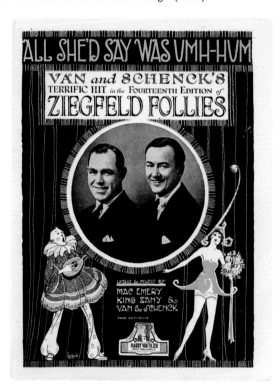

Oh! Mister Gallagher and Mister Shean
Vaudevillians Ed Gallagher and Al Shean not only made their names famous, but also provided the comic hit of the year when they sang this song in *Ziegfeld's Follies of 1922*. The song was a series of provocative questions and answers that could be varied to fit any current topic, and were frequently outrageous. (1922)

Oh! Gee, Oh! Gosh, Oh! Golly I'm in Love
Eddie Cantor, known as "Banjo Eyes," worked in vaudeville before joining the *Ziegfeld Follies* where he became one of the main attractions with his singing, dancing, and comedy flair. Cantor respected Ziegfeld as a showman and worked in other Ziegfeld productions besides the *Follies* and *Midnight Frolic* editions. He was a big hit in *Whoopee* singing the provocative title song by Gus Kahn and Walter Donaldson. (1923)

Everybody Loves My Baby
Ann Pennington was small in stature (under five feet), but big in talent. The pert and vivacious dancer was the epitome of the Jazz Baby, and did the shimmy and the black bottom in editions of *George White's Scandals* before appearing in *Ziegfeld's Follies*. She featured this song by Spencer Williams and Jack Palmer in *Ziegfeld Follies of 1924*.

Love Is Like That
Ruth Etting was a well-known singer and recording star when Ziegfeld featured her in his 1927 *Follies* singing Irving Berlin's "Shaking the Blues Away." She was especially talented at singing torch songs, and appeared in three more *Follies* parlaying each of her songs into all-time hits. (1931)

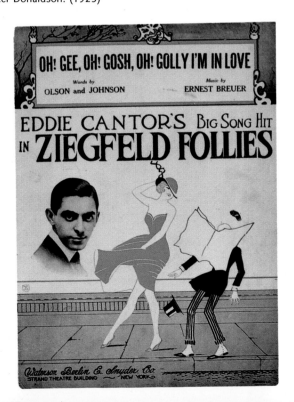

36

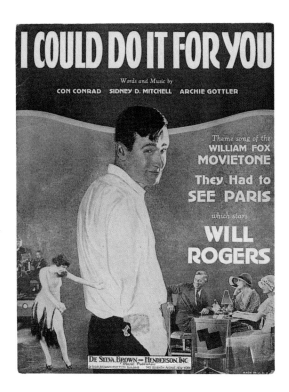

I Could Do It for You
Will Rogers was a popular Ziegfeld entertainer from 1916 to 1924. He was a one-time cowhand and trick roper who added homespun humor to his act, amusing audiences with his wry, incisive, down-home commentary that lampooned politicians and current events. Ziegfeld gave him a free hand with his act, and Rogers didn't let him down. He is seen here on the cover of a song from one of his early sound movies. (1929)

Oh Gee; Oh Joy!
Marilyn Miller was a favorite of Mr. Ziegfeld who mounted this special production of *Rosalie* for her with top show business talents contributing the music. This song was composed by George Gershwin with lyrics by brother Ira and P. G. Wodehouse. (1928)

Two Loves
Gifted torch singer Helen Morgan is photographed in an alluring yellow satin gown trimmed with sumptuous fur. Fresh from her success as Julie in Jerome Kern's *Show Boat*, she sang in Ziegfeld's last *Follies'* production before his death a year later. (1931)

The House Is Haunted
Ziegfeld's widow, Billie Burke, produced this *Follies* purportedly to pay off Ziegfeld's huge debts. Though it lacked the glitter of the former shows, it had beautiful girls aplenty and a good roster of stars including Fannie Brice, Eve Arden, Buddy Ebsen, and Jane Froman that attracted audiences for a six month run. (1934)

Passing Show
and Other Pre-1920 Revues

The *Passing Show* revue, based on an earlier undistinguished revue in 1894, was started in 1912 by theatrical entrepreneurs and producers the Shubert brothers (Jacob, Lee, and Sam). They owned the Winter Garden, one of the largest theaters in New York City, and presented the *Passing Show of 1912* as a summer entertainment. It was successful in attracting audiences, and it became an annual event similar to Ziegfeld's *Follies*. It consisted of song and dance numbers and comedy routines about current events and local celebrities.

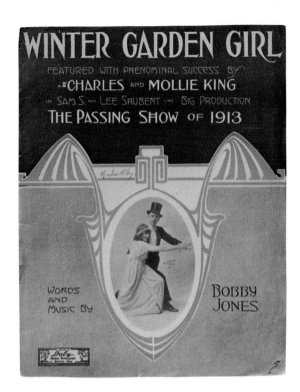

Winter Garden Girl
The Passing Show of 1913 featured this song written by Bobby Jones in tribute to the beautiful showgirls appearing at the Winter Garden. It was performed in the production by the cover stars Charles and Mollie King. (1914)

The Wedding Glide
The Passing Show of 1912 took the name of its 1894 predecessor, but was much more ambitious. Eighty show girls and long-legged Charlotte Greenwood appeared in this first edition staged at the Winter Garden. The show included songs by Louis A. Hirsch like this one that borrowed some of its theme from Mendelssohn's Wedding March. (1912)

Passing Show revues were rich in talent. The first act in *Passing Show of 1912* contained the song "Ragtime Jockey Man" by a relatively unknown rehearsal pianist named Irving Berlin. The shows continued into the 1920s, and through the years presented such brilliant stars as Charlotte Greenwood, Marilyn Miller, Fred and Adele Astaire, and Fred Allen.

Pretty Baby
This hit song from *The Passing Show of 1916* was written by Gus Kahn with music by Tony Jackson and Egbert Van Alstyne. It was sung by Dolly Hackett in the production. (1916)

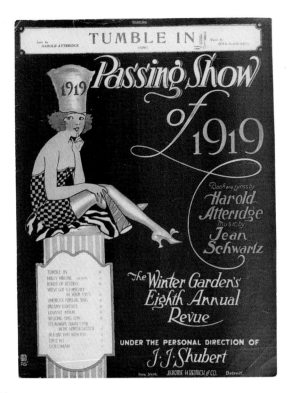

Tumble In
The Shubert Brothers produced one *Passing Show* revue a year in late spring, running through the summer. The shows used talented actors and comedians, good music, and pretty girls, and were very popular, giving the *Ziegfeld Follies* some healthy competition. This song from *Passing Show of 1919* was written by Harold Atteridge with music by Jean Schwartz. (1919)

Land of My Heart's Desire
The first of *George White's Scandals* patterned itself after *Ziegfeld's Follies*, and was an instant success, running for 128 performances. George White, himself, appeared in the production along with shimmy dancer Ann Pennington, comedian Lou Holtz, and the usual complement of beautiful girls. (1919)

Rock-a-Bye Your Baby with a Dixie Melody
Al Jolson introduced this song with his customary exuberance in the popular extravaganza *Sinbad*, a Shubert show at the Winter Garden that ran for a healthy 388 performances. He was one of the stage's most charismatic performers, and loved his audiences to the extent that he had a special runway built that brought him closer to the people. (1918) *Collection of E. J. Hannan*

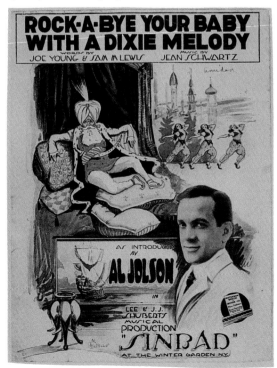

Red, Red as a Rose
Britisher John Murray Anderson staged this first *Greenwich Village Follies* at the small Greenwich Village Theatre in New York. It broke away from the chorus girl syndrome that dominated other revues, and brought a fresh aura of sophistication to musical theater. Music was composed by A. Baldwin Sloane. (1919)

Songs from Musical Revues
of the 1920s

The revue was at its peak in the 1920s as was Broadway musical theater in general; 1927 offered an astounding 268 shows. In this age of Prohibition with its free-and-easy flappers and bathtub gin, some of the revues became racier. An annual series called *Artists and Models* started in 1923, and went a step further than Ziegfeld's exhibitionism with its display of promenading showgirls with naked breasts, appealing to largely stag audiences. Shows at the gargantuan Hippodrome theater were vaudevillian in concept, sometimes drawing from the circus world for spectacle in the use of elephants and clowns. Also competing with the *Ziegfeld Follies* and *The Passing Show* were other variety revues like *Greenwich Village Follies*, *George White's Scandals*, and *Music Box Revues* that attracted their share of audiences, and contributed many great songs to the literature.

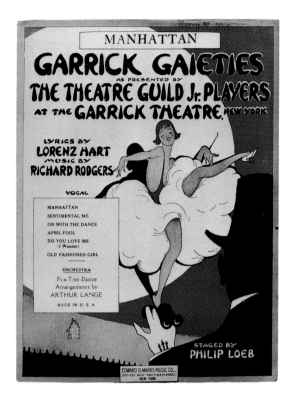

Manhattan
The first edition of *Garrick Gaieties*, presented by the Theatre Guild, was well received, owing in part to the fresh and original music provided by the new young team of Lorenz Hart and Richard Rodgers. This song from the show became one of their first popular hits. Like a breath of fresh air, it was a total break with the light opera tradition of the Sigmund Romberg school, moving in a new direction of typical American informality. (1925)

My Golden Dream Ship
Post-war optimism bloomed in revues like *Better Times*, a spectacular vaudeville show produced by Charles Dillingham at the New York Hippodrome. The Hippodrome shows were bigger and more lavish than ever, and this show offered exotic live animals on stage, beautiful girls perched on a huge lighted fan, and a Ladies' Jazz band to please jazz-loving theatergoers. (1921)

Mountain Greenery
A second edition of *Garrick Gaieties* again featured songs by Rodgers and Hart, and satirical comedy that ribbed George Bernard Shaw, Gilbert and Sullivan, and mocked conventional musical theater. (1926)

Climbing Up the Ladder of Love
Earl Carroll's revues relied heavily on gorgeous girls, lavish scenery, and low-brow comedy acts, but drew audiences in to view the lovely ladies. (1926)

Pickin' Cotton
George White's ninth edition of his *Scandals* benefited greatly from the songs of B. G. De Sylva, Lew Brown, and Ray Henderson including this rhythmic ditty about happy cotton pickers in the South. (1928)

All Alone Monday
Fanny Brice starred in this edition of *Hollywood Music Box Revue* presented for the first time at Louis O. Macloon's Music Box Theatre in Hollywood, California. Her pensive rendition of this song with words by Bert Kalmar and music by Harry Ruby was the hit of the show. (1926)

Once in a Lifetime
This 7th edition of *Earl Carroll Vanities* continued to exploit feminine pulchritude to the delight of audiences, and also threw in the comedy of W. C. Fields, the music of Vincent Lopez's band, with dances and ensembles provided by Busby Berkeley. (1928)

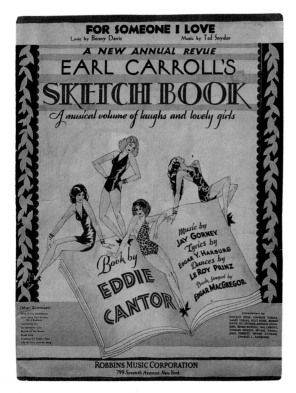

Songs from Musical Revues
of the 1930s

In the 1930s, revue series like the *Follies*, the *Scandals*, and the *Vanities* were still around, joined by the first *Little Show* in 1929 with songs like "I Guess I'll Have to Change My Plan," Fred Allen's wry humor, and Clifton Webb's dancing. Second and third *Little Shows* met with less success. With the country in the throes of the Depression, many of the revues satirized political figures and current events which was the vogue for a time, but they failed to flourish after the 1930s. Audiences were beginning to prefer more mature musical offerings, shows with both a good strong story line and good music.

For Someone I Love
Earl Carroll renamed his *Vanities* revue to *Earl Carroll's Sketchbook*, this time enlisting the aid of Eddie Cantor who wrote the book. The show featured song interpolations by a raft of big names including Benny Davis, Ted Snyder, Irving Kahal, Vincent Rose, and Charles and Harry Tobias, among others. (1929)

I May Be Wrong
John Murray Anderson was a Broadway impresario who made his reputation with his mounting of the *Greenwich Village Follies* revues. He compiled and staged his own successful *Murray Anderson's Almanac* featuring this song with words by Harry Ruskin and music by Henry Sullivan, performed by Trixie Friganza and Jimmie Savo in the show. (1929)

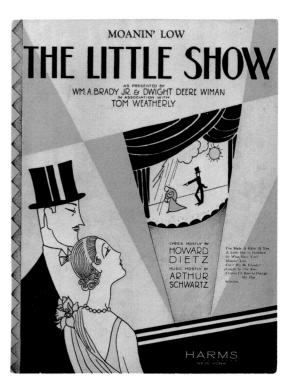

Moanin' Low
The Little Show was a polished production of more sophistication than usually found in a Broadway revue. "Moanin' Low," with words by Ralph Rainger and music by Arthur Schwartz, was effectively moaned with great pathos by Libby Holman. (1929)

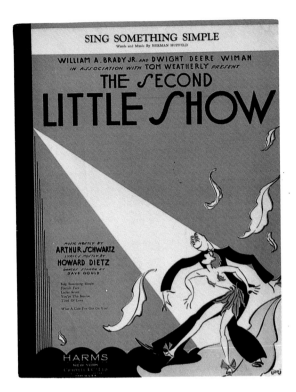

Sing Something Simple
Following the success of its predecessor, *The Second Little Show* appeared in 1930. Herman Hupfeld, best known for his song "As Time Goes By," wrote this song performed by Ruth Tester in the show. (1930)

Mad Dogs and Englishmen
The Third Little Show was called "The Aristocrat of All Revues." Noel Coward wrote the clever lyrics and music for this featured song performed by Beatrice Lillie. (1931)

Dancing in the Dark
Fred and Adele Astaire are two of the faces that appear on artist John Held Jr.'s caricature figures drawn on song covers from the stage revue *The Band Wagon*. (1931)

Exactly Like You
The show's producer, Lew Leslie, had a number of prior hit shows including the famous *Blackbirds* revues, but his *International Revue* was less successful. This song written by Dorothy Fields and Jimmy McHugh for the show became a popular success as did a second number, "On the Sunny Side of the Street." (1930)

Louisiana Hayride
Howard Dietz and Arthur Schwartz wrote the music and lyrics for *Flying Colors*, a Max Gordon production that featured Charles Butterworth, Clifton Webb, Patsy Kelly, and the dancing of Buddy and Vilma Ebsen to choreography by Agnes DeMille. Other good songs from the show were "Alone Together" and "A Shine on Your Shoes." (1932)

Posin'
This syncopated song by Sammy Cahn and Saul Chaplin was featured in the first edition of Ed Fox's *New Grand Terrace Revue* showcasing the talents of American bandleader, composer, and pianist Fletcher Henderson. (1937)

44

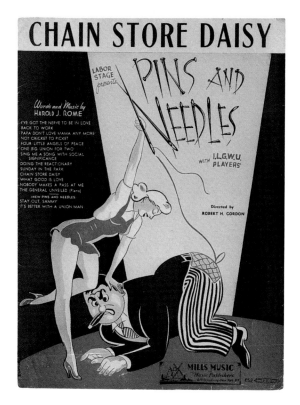

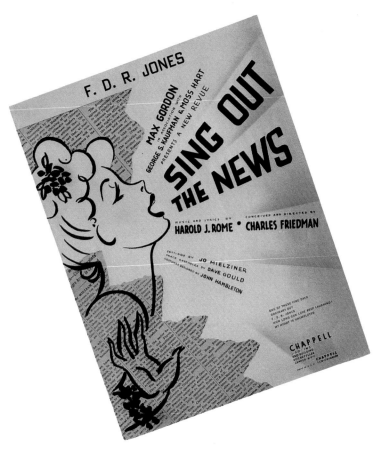

Chain Store Daisy
Pins and Needles, with a cast composed of talented members of the International Ladies Garment Workers' Union, was a great satirical success lampooning unions, politics, and current social problems. Timely songs by Harold J. Rome included "It's Not Cricket to Picket," "Sing Me a Song with Social Significance" and "Four Little Angels of Peace" with comic characterizations of Chamberlain, Mussolini, Hitler, and a Japanese statesman. The show was a modestly mounted production in a small theater with simple scenery and two-piano accompaniment, but ran for 1,108 performances. (1938)

F. D. R. Jones
Max Gordon in conjunction with George S. Kaufman and Moss Hart produced *Sing Out the News*, patterned after the successful *Pins and Needles* revue. It too had songs by Harold Rome with commentary about Franklin Roosevelt's New Deal philosophy, but the show lacked the pizzazz of *Pins and Needles* and closed after 105 performances. (1938)

Love, I'd Give My Life for You
The *Hollywood Revue Production* was staged by Bobby Sanford on Broadway in 1938-39. It featured a bevy of glamorous beauties and songs by Dave Oppenheim, Al Jacobs, and Jack Palmer. (1938)

45

I LOVE A PIANO
CHAS. B. DILLINGHAM presents
GABY DESLYS
in a new Musical Comedy
STOP! LOOK! LISTEN!
THAT HULA HULA . . $ .60
I LOVE A PIANO 60
THE GIRL ON THE MAGAZINE 60
EVERYTHING in AMERICA IS RAGTIME . . .60
WHEN I GET BACK TO THE U. S. A. 60
STOP, LOOK, LISTEN . . .60
TEACH ME HOW TO LOVE 60
FATHER WANTED ME to LEARN A TRADE .60
BLOW YOUR HORN . . .60
SAILOR SONG 60
I LOVE TO DANCE 60
WHEN I'M OUT WITH YOU 60
THE LAW MUST BE OBEYED 60
SELECTION 1.00
BOOK BY
HARRY B. SMITH
STAGED BY
R.H. BURNSIDE
LYRICS & MUSIC
BY
IRVING BERLIN
PUBLISHED BY
IRVING BERLIN INC.
BARBELLE

CHAPTER 3:
THE BIG FIVE
(OR SIX OR SEVEN!)

Victor Herbert (1859-1924)

I Want to Be a Good Lamb
Victor Herbert was a strong influence on the American theater from the dawn of the twentieth century until his death in 1924. Though many of his operettas seem dated today, his songs continue to delight and inspire, and remain in the repertoire. *Collection of Harold Jacobs*

Opposite page:
I Love a Piano
This song from the musical show *Stop! Look! Listen!* was a sensational production number with the entire stage designed as a giant piano keyboard with six pianists playing the refrain simultaneously on six pianos. The show starred French actress Gaby Deslys who appears on the colorful song cover by Barbelle. (1915)

Victor Herbert and George M. Cohan were two outstanding composers of theater music during the first decade of the twentieth century. Though they were worlds apart in their expression and technique, they each had a trend-setting impact on the future of American musical theater. The thread of Herbert's European romanticism can be followed to the later romanticism of *My Fair Lady*. Similarly, the tradition of Cohan's brash, flag-waving, fast-paced musicals is carried on in later shows *Hello, Dolly* and *The Music Man*. Each in his own way made a contribution of real value to American music.

Herbert was born in Ireland in 1859, and had a thorough musical education in Stuttgart, Germany. He played many instruments well, but was most proficient on the cello. Frank Damrosch, a talent scout for the New York Metropolitan Opera, discovered Herbert's wife, an operatic soprano in Stuttgart, and both she and her husband were lured to New York where she sang and he played in the orchestra. Herbert established his musical reputation in America when his cello concerto was performed by the New York Philharmonic in 1887. He subsequently became conductor of the Pittsburgh Symphony Orchestra from 1898-1904.

Herbert's first light opera, *Prince Ananias*, was written in 1892, followed by a prodigious output of operettas in a career that brought him worldwide fame. He and his wife became naturalized Americans, and his music metamorphosed from the Viennese tradition of light opera into a style that stayed in favor with the American public long after the Viennese import expired. The songs of Victor Herbert, once heard, are not soon forgotten. They possess a unique quality of emotional classicism that strikes a chord of response in the hearts of his audience.

Naughty Marietta (1910), with book and lyrics by Rida Johnson Young, is considered by many to be Herbert's greatest triumph. He produced an extraordinary array of hit songs in this show including "Ah, Sweet Mystery of Life," "Tramp, Tramp, Tramp," "I'm Falling In Love With Someone," and "Italian Street Song." Other popular Herbert shows were *Sweethearts* (1913), *The Only Girl* (1914), and *Orange Blossoms* (1922).

Victor Herbert Show Songs

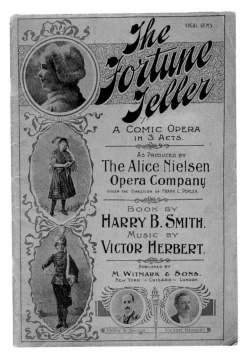

The Fortune Teller Vocal Gems
Herbert's music and Harry B. Smith's libretto were an inspired combination for *The Fortune Teller* written expressly for soprano Alice Neilsen. Her hit songs were "Always Do As People Say You Should" and "Romany Life." Eugene Cowles sang the outstanding song hit of the show, "Gypsy Love Song," to her in the play. (1898)

Toyland
Babes In Toyland, with book and lyrics by Glen MacDonough, was a big hit for Victor Herbert with this lilting song and other memorable pieces—"March of the Toys" and the children's chorus, "I Can't Do the Sum." (1903)

If I Were on the Stage (Kiss Me)
Fritzi Scheff was the star of *Mlle. Modiste* singing the Victor Herbert song that was forever afterwards associated with her, "Kiss Me Again." Henry Blossom was praised for the literacy and fluency of his book and lyrics. (1905)

The Streets of New York
The famous comedy team Fred Stone and Dave Montgomery co-starred in this successful collaboration of Victor Herbert and Henry Blossom, *The Red Mill*, which ran on Broadway for 274 performances. The score contained many hit songs including "Because You're You," "In Old New York," and "Every Day Is Ladies Day with Me." (1906)

48

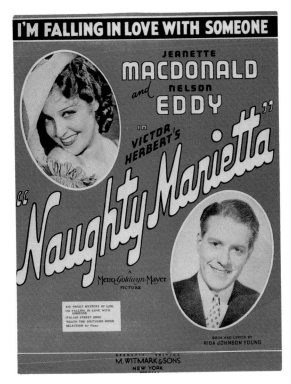

I'm Falling in Love with Someone
Victor Herbert's wonderful songs from the operetta *Naughty Marietta* enjoyed renewed popularity in the 1930s when soprano Jeanette MacDonald and baritone Nelson Eddy sang them in the Metro-Goldwyn-Mayer movie. (1934)

George M. Cohan (1878-1942)

I Was Born in Virginia
George M. Cohan wrote this song for the hit musical show *George Washington Jr.* He was actually born in Providence, Rhode Island. Other of his more famous song titles are shown on the cover. (1933 reprint of 1906 song)

George M. Cohan, nicknamed the "Yankee Doodle Dandy," was born in 1878 to a theatrical family. The Four Cohans' vaudeville act consisted of young George Michael, sister Josephine, and parents Jerry and Helen. George appeared in the family act on Broadway at an early age, and before long was writing songs and material for them. In 1901 twenty-two year old George wrote and composed the music for his first full-blown musical comedy, *The Governor's Son.* This started him on a long career as an actor, songwriter, playwright, and producer that ultimately led to the White House and the award of the Congressional Medal of Honor.

The Governor's Son (Gems from)
The Four Cohans starred in Cohan's first Broadway show *The Governor's Son.* Also appearing was Ethel Levey, who became Cohan's first wife. The show opened on Broadway to lukewarm reviews, and ran for only 32 New York performances. (1901)

Cohan's impressive Broadway credits include the production of twenty-two musical shows and thirteen plays, with his top successes mainly in the first decade of the twentieth century. His second effort *Running For Office* opened in 1903, but was only moderately successful. His first real hit came with *Little Johnny Jones* in 1904, with such patriotic and exultant tunes as "The Yankee Doodle Boy" and "Give My Regards to Broadway."

Cohan's settings and characters were refreshingly American, a welcome respite from the prevalent European comic opera, and the emphasis of his music was on patriotism. He loved his country and indulged in "waving the American flag" at every opportunity. As one of the characters remarked in the biographical movie, *Yankee Doodle Dandy,* "He's the whole darn country squeezed into one pair of pants!"

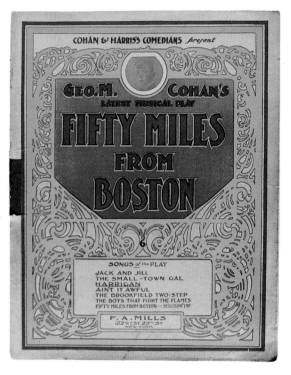

The Yankee Doodle Boy
Young George M. Cohan not only wrote the book, lyrics, and music, but he also starred in his first successful Broadway show *Little Johnny Jones*. This song became closely identified with him through his long career, and he was "The Yankee Doodle Boy." (1904)

Harrigan
This jolly hit song from Cohan's *Fifty Miles from Boston* capitalized on the catchy spelling trick, "H-A-Double R-I-G-A-N spells Harrigan." (1907)

Mary's a Grand Old Name
Producers Klaw and Erlanger backed Cohan's show *Forty-Five Minutes from Broadway* that also contained hit songs "So Long, Mary," the title song, and the mildly profane "Stand Up and Fight Like Hell." Cohan wasn't in the cast, giving the leading role to Victor Moore. Audiences applauded popular singer Fay Templeton's rendition of this song. (1905)

You're a Grand Old Flag
George Washington Jr. brought Cohan back to the stage as the star of this show that he wrote and produced. The song was originally called "You're a Grand Old Rag," but some found it offensive and Cohan quickly changed the title and withdrew the initial sheet music. The original with "rag" in the title is, of course, a prime collectible. (1906)

Jerome Kern, born in New York, had a strong musical background, learning piano from his mother at an early age, and studying harmony for a year at the New York College of Music. In his teens he went to Germany for further studies in music theory and composition at the Heidelberg Conservatory. His first published piece was a piano solo "At the Casino" (1902) released by the Lyceum Publishing Company. It wasn't especially notable, but nonetheless a feather in the cap of the budding 17-year old composer.

Kern's ambition was to become a composer for the theater. In 1904 he was befriended by the powerful Max Dreyfus, president of the T. B. Harms music publishing firm, a man of considerable influence on Broadway. Dreyfus was impressed by Kern, and saw that two of his songs were interpolated into the Broadway show *An English Daisy*. Interpolation of songs into musical scores was established procedure in show business at the time, and Kern contributed almost one hundred melodies into thirty Broadway musicals between 1905 and 1912. He composed his first complete score in 1911 for *The Red Petticoat* that ran for 61 performances.

Over There
This stirring World War I song by George M. Cohan was a gigantic hit published in many different editions. Cohan's life and career was the subject of the Warner Brothers motion picture *Yankee Doodle Dandy* starring James Cagney portraying Cohan. (1942)

Jerome Kern (1885-1945)

Meet Jerome Kern at the Piano
The incomparable Jerome Kern appears on the cover of a song folio that contains some of his most famous hit songs.

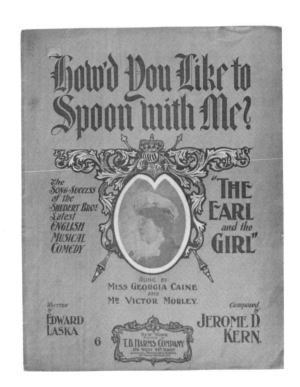

How'd You Like to Spoon With Me?
This early piece by Kern was first used as an interpolation in Ivan Caryll's show *The Earl and the Girl*. The song's reception was no doubt helped by its performance by a group of beauties who sang it while on swings soaring out over the heads of the first few rows of the audience. (1905)

Kern's first recognition as a composer of real stature came with his song "They Didn't Believe Me" used in *The Girl From Utah* in 1914. He had found his own style and from then on was recognized as one of Broadway's most gifted composers. *Show Boat* in 1927 is considered by many to be Kern's masterpiece, breaking new ground in theater history with its mature story line and superb cohesion of story and song.

Kern also wrote successfully for the screen. The show *Roberta* was transferred from stage to cinema with songs "Lovely to Look At," "Smoke Gets in Your Eyes," and "Yesterday." *Show Boat* was kept alive through three movie adaptations, the first in 1929 starring Laura La Plante and Joseph Schildkraut, the second in 1936 with Irene Dunne and Allan Jones, and the 1951 version with Kathryn Grayson and Howard Keel. The 1936 movie *Swing Time* with Fred Astaire and Ginger Rogers featured wonderful Kern songs with lyrics by Dorothy Field including the unforgettable "The Way You Look Tonight" which won Kern an Academy Award. Kern's music with words by Ira Gershwin, including the haunting "Long Ago and Far Away," ensured the success of the movie *Cover Girl* (1942) co-starring Rita Hayworth and Gene Kelly.

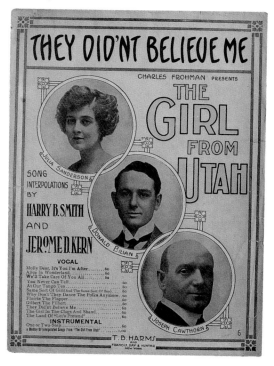

They Didn't Believe Me
Jerome Kern's first great hit was composed to words by M. E. Rourke, and sung by Julia Sanderson in the Ruben/Jones musical *The Girl from Utah*. His harmonic inventiveness and melodic gifts established him as one of the foremost composers for the musical theater. (1914)

Bill
Originally written for *Oh Lady! Lady!*, this song didn't work out during tryouts and was dropped from the show. Years later it was revived for *Show Boat* with modifications to the lyrics by Oscar Hammerstein II, and sung by the inimitable Helen Morgan. This original large size edition with cover illustration by Malcolm Strauss is the more valuable because of its rarity. (1918)

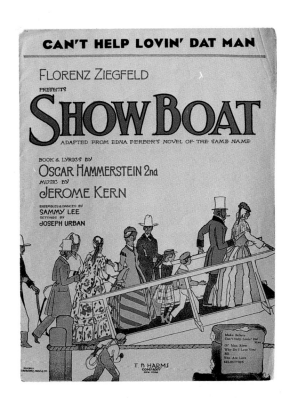

Can't Help Lovin' Dat Man
Kern's crowning achievement was *Show Boat*. It had a strong story line based on Edna Ferber's novel that probed the social problems of an interracial marriage, and it had Kern's incomparable music with lyrics by Oscar Hammerstein 2nd—songs that became blockbuster hits. Helen Morgan sang this in the original production. (1927)

When Jerome Kern died in 1945 President Truman spoke for America when he said:

"I am among the grateful millions who have played and listened to the music of Jerome Kern, and I wish to be among those of his fellow Americans who pay him tribute today. His melodies will live in our voices and warm our hearts for many years to come, for they are the kind of simple, honest songs that belong to no time or fashion. The man who gave them to us earned a lasting place in his nation's memory."

Jerome Kern Show Songs

Smoke Gets in Your Eyes
Roberta was a huge success with great Kern songs composed with lyrics by Otto Harbach. Tamara Drasin sang this song in the show, vaudeville's aging Fay Templeton performed "Yesterdays," and a budding comedian Bob Hope made his mark. (1933)

In Love With Love
Talented Fred Stone and his daughter Dorothy starred in *The Stepping Stones* with songs composed by Jerome Kern to lyrics by Anne Caldwell. An accomplished actor, comedian, singer, and dancer, Stone started out in a vaudeville act with David Montgomery as Montgomery and Stone, then continued his stage success after his partner's death. (1923)

All the Things You Are
Very Warm for May played for only 59 performances despite a cast that included Vera-Ellen, June Allyson, Eve Arden, and Donald Brian with production by Max Gordon and Vincente Minnelli. This song has lived on as a great Kern/Hammerstein II classic. (1939)

Irving Berlin (1888-1989)

Remember
A youthful Irving Berlin appears on the sheet music cover of one of his haunting waltzes. (1925)

1. The melody should be within the range of most singers.
2. The title should be attention-getting, and should be repeated within the song.
3. The song should be able to be sung by either a man or a woman.
4. The song requires "heart interest."
5. It should be original in idea, words, and music.
6. Stick to nature—homely, concrete, and everyday, not as an abstraction.
7. Use open vowels in the lyrics for euphonious sound.
8. Make the song as simple as possible.
9. The songwriter must regard his work as a business, and to be successful he must work and work, and then WORK.

Significant contributions by Berlin to musical theater included his World War I soldier show *Yip-Yip-Yaphank* with songs "Mandy" and "Oh, How I Hate to Get Up in the Morning," several editions of *Ziegfeld Follies*, his *Music Box Revues* from 1921 to 1924, and complete scores for other hit Broadway shows. He received many accolades for his music including the Medal of Merit for his World War II fund-raising stage and screen musical *This Is the Army*, the Congressional Gold Medal for "God Bless America," an Academy Award for "White Christmas," the French Legion of Honor, and a Grammy Lifetime Achievement Award.

Irving Berlin Songs

Someone once asked Jerome Kern where in American music he would place Irving Berlin, to which Mr. Kern replied, "Irving Berlin *is* American music." Another admirer, George Gershwin, characterized him as "America's Franz Schubert" for his incredible genius at song writing.

Irving Berlin was born Israel Baline in Mohilev, Russia in 1888, the youngest child of a black-bearded Russian rabbi. The family emigrated to New York in 1893, little knowing that young Izzy would make for himself such a special place in American music, not just for his theater music but for his contribution to the whole realm of popular music.

Berlin started out writing only the lyrics for songs because he couldn't read music, but he taught himself to pick out little tunes on the piano, and used an arranger to write them down and harmonize them. He eventually learned to play the piano using only the black keys, and had a special piano which was mechanically altered to transpose.

Of particular interest are Irving Berlin's nine rules for writing popular songs which he offered in an interview with *The American Magazine*. That he followed his own advice is evident in the phenomenal success of his songs through the years. In his long career, he wrote as many as fifteen hundred popular songs, some published under other names.

Marie from Sunny Italy
This was Berlin's first published song for which he wrote the lyrics and Nick Nicholson wrote the music. His share of the royalties was said to be thirty-seven cents, and ironically the same piece today brings many hundreds of dollars at auctions. (1907)

Settle Down in a One-Horse Town
Berlin's first complete musical score was written for *Watch Your Step*, a light-hearted show starring popular dancers Irene and Vernon Castle. The hit show ran for 175 performances. Berlin subsequently composed the scores for sixteen more Broadway shows. (1914)

You'd Be Surprised
Ziegfeld Follies of 1919 featured seven Irving Berlin songs including "Mandy," "A Pretty Girl Is Like a Melody," and this comically wry song that was put over by Eddie Cantor in the show. Cantor later made a hit recording on the Emerson label that sold over 800,000 copies. (1919)

When My Baby Smiles
Fresh out of the Army in 1919, Irving Berlin with partner Max Winslow started the Irving Berlin Music Publishing firm at 1587 Broadway in New York City. This engaging tune was one of the first in his catalog. Small globe in lower right corner has logo describing Standards of the World—"Sterling on Silver," and "Irving Berlin on Songs." (1919)

What'll I Do
Berlin, with partner Sam Harris, opened up The Music Box theater on Broadway in 1921 which successfully showcased his songs. This plaintive hit was first introduced by Grace Moore in the third *Music Box Revue* in 1923. It was published in early 1924 and sold over a million copies of sheet music.

Blue Skies
Singer Belle Baker needed a good song for the Ziegfeld show *Betsy*, and implored her friend Irving Berlin to come up with something the night before the opening. "Blue Skies" was the result, and though the show was panned, the song was wildly received, and she sang 24 encores, aided in the last by Berlin himself who was in the audience. (1927)

Give Me Your Tired, Your Poor
For his show *Miss Liberty*, Irving Berlin was inspired to write music for the eloquent words of Emma Lazarus that are inscribed on the Statue of Liberty. He loved this song, and predicted it would become as big a hit as "God Bless America," which it failed to do. (1949)

Marrying for Love
Ethel Merman starred in Berlin's *Call Me Madam* in a role tailor-made for her talents, a society leader who is truly "The Hostess With the Most-es' on the Ball," as the song goes. The show's character was based on the real-life ambassador Perle Mesta who was famous for her Washington parties. Peter Arno, distinctive artist for sophisticated *New Yorker* magazine, did the cover caricature of Ethel Merman. (1950)

Easter Parade
The big hit of Irving Berlin's show *As Thousands Cheer* was "Easter Parade," a tune he had written fifteen years earlier for an unsuccessful song "Smile and Show Your Dimple." In this resurrection it became a showstopper when introduced by Marilyn Miller and Clifton Webb in the festive parade at the end of the first act. (1933)

George Gershwin (1898-1937)

The Gershwins
Special thanks to W. English Strunsky for the photo of George Gershwin that appears on the jacket of *The Gershwins* biography prepared by Robert Kimball and Alfred Simon. (1973)

George Gershwin was born in Brooklyn, the son of poor Jewish parents, Rose and Morris Gershovitz (who changed their name first to Gershvin then to Gershwin). He was the second of four children. When a secondhand upright piano was brought into the family apartment, twelve-year-old George immediately displayed his innate talent by sitting down at the keyboard and playing a popular tune of the day. His aptitude did not go unnoticed, and he was provided with lessons, eventually studying with a classical teacher who introduced him to the music of Chopin, Liszt, and Debussy, and who also saw that he was instructed in basic harmony and theory.

George became a brilliant pianist, and dropped out of high school when he was fifteen to go to work for the Jerome H. Remick Music Publishing Company as a piano pounding song plugger. When he was eighteen years old, his first song was published by the Harry Von Tilzer Music Publishing Company, with lyrics by Murray Roth, "When You Want 'Em, You Can't Get 'Em."

As a sideline George made piano rolls for the Standard Music Company's Perfection label and for the Universal label. He used not only his own name but the pseudonyms James Baker, Fred Murtha, and Bert Wynn. He is believed to have made 125 piano rolls, of which 80 are thought to be still in existence.

Gershwin was a great admirer of Jerome Kern's music, and said many years later that he followed Kern's work closely, and studied each song that he composed. With his discovery of Kern's music he became conscious of the fine direction that musical comedy was taking, and was inspired to be a part of its artistic growth.

While composing musical comedies, George also turned out serious jazz compositions. In 1924 after a brief and unsuccessful experiment in the *Scandals of 1922* with the one-act jazz opera *Blue Monday* (later called *135th Street*), Gershwin composed "Rhapsody in Blue" which established him as a serious symphonic jazz composer as well as a popular songwriter. Other important works followed: "Piano Concerto in F," "An American in Paris," "Second Rhapsody," "Cuban Overture," and his impressive folk opera *Porgy and Bess*, written in collaboration with Ira Gershwin and DuBose Heyward in 1935.

After *Porgy and Bess* Gershwin went to Hollywood to work on film music. His movie scores included *The Sunshine Trail* (1923), *Delicious* (1931), and two delightful Fred Astaire movies—*Shall We Dance* and *A Damsel In Distress* (1937). While working in Hollywood on the score for *Goldwyn Follies* he fell ill and died of a brain tumor at age thirty-eight leaving a legacy of memorable show tunes and exciting serious jazz compositions. His musical comedy songs captured the essence of 1920s and '30s musical theater, and his classical compositions remain timeless contributions to serious music.

George Gershwin Show Songs

Nobody But You
Gershwin's first complete Broadway show score was for *La La Lucille*. This particular tune was composed as early as 1913, fragments of which were found in one of Gershwin's early music exercise notebooks. Lyrics by Arthur Jackson and B. G. DeSylva. (1919)

Do It Again
This hit song from the musical *The French Doll* was composed by George with lyrics by B. G. DeSylva. Irene Bordoni introduced it in the show. (1922)

Oh, Lady Be Good
The first complete score by George and Ira Gershwin together was for the smash hit *Lady Be Good* starring Fred and Adele Astaire. "The Man I Love" was sung by Adele Astaire during the tryout run in Philadelphia, but was dropped from the show, later to reappear briefly in *Strike Up the Band*. (1924)

Somebody Loves Me
This great popular classic was composed by George with words by Buddy DeSylva and Ballard Macdonald for the 1924 *George White Scandals* revue. It was sung by Winnie Lightner in the show. From 1920 to 1924 Gershwin regularly wrote music for the *Scandals* including the famous "I'll Build a Stairway to Paradise" for which his brother Ira wrote the lyrics under the pen name of Arthur Francis. (1924)

Someone to Watch over Me
George and Ira Gershwin collaborated on this soulful ballad that was introduced in *Oh, Kay!* by Gertrude Lawrence who sang it while holding a rag doll. Other well-known Gershwin songs from this show were "Clap Yo' Hands" and "Do, Do, Do." (1926)

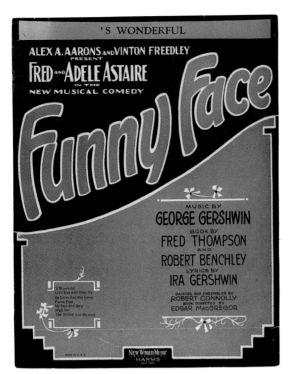

'S Wonderful
This Gershwin brothers' song from the musical *Funny Face* was introduced by Adele Astaire and Allen Kearns. Ira Gershwin violated one of the cardinal rules in lyric writing, to avoid emphasis on the sibilant "s," but he brought it off successfully. (1927)

Of Thee I Sing
Of Thee I Sing was a musical satire on presidential elections with music by the Gershwin brothers. It ran for 441 performances, and popular hits from the show include this song and "Love Is Sweeping the Country." Highly praised by critics, it garnered a Pulitzer Prize for best play of the year. (1931)

I Got Rhythm
Girl Crazy was notable, not only for its hit Gershwin songs, but for introducing Ethel Merman to Broadway. She went down in show business history for her boisterous rendition of this song in which she dazzled her audience by holding one high note for sixteen bars. Other solid hits from the show were "Bidin' My Time," "Embraceable You," and "But Not for Me." (1930)

Summertime
DuBose Heyward wrote the lyrics for George Gershwin's touching lullaby sung by Abbie Mitchell in the first performance of the opera *Porgy and Bess*. Other unforgettable songs from the show include "It Ain't Necessarily So," "I Got Plenty O' Nothin'," and "Bess, You Is My Woman Now." (1935)

59

Cole Porter (1891-1964)

Cole Porter Song Album
A photograph of Cole Porter adorns the cover of this song folio that features some of his song hits through the years.

Cole Porter merits inclusion in a list of big five musical show composers for the consistent excellence of his songs, for his unique ability to match lyrics to music, and for the constant delight and pleasure that his songs have contributed to the world.

Porter was born in Peru, Indiana, to a well-to-do farming family. His early musical abilities were recognized, and he was given piano and violin lessons to foster his talents. The family expected him to become a lawyer and he indulged their plans by entering Harvard Law School. But after a year studying law, he followed his natural bent and switched to the School of Music. He composed his first complete score in 1916 for *See America First* which folded after fifteen performances. After a stint in the French Foreign Legion in 1917, Porter returned to America and wrote what became his first hit song, "Old Fashioned Garden," which was used in the 1919 revue *Hitchy-Koo*.

Returning to Paris in 1920 he studied serious music at the Schola Cantorum—harmony, counterpoint, orchestration, and the classics. But he eventually realized that his true calling was to the world of popular music. He continued to write songs for revues, and scored another hit with "I'm in Love Again" for the 1924 *Greenwich Village Follies*. By 1930 Cole Porter's reputation as a sophisticated song smith was well established.

Cole Porter Show Songs

Old Fashioned Garden
Porter received critical accolades for his musical contributions to the 1919 *Hitchy-Koo* revue. The show only had 52 performances, but this song is considered Porter's first bona fide popular song. (1919)

Let's Do It
Irene Bordoni sang this Cole Porter song with its clever suggestive lyrics in the show *Paris*. The audience enjoyed the double entendre suggestion about all the species that "do it," and the song became an immediate hit. (1928)

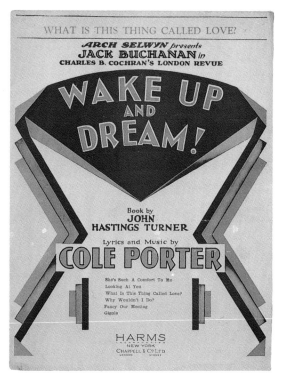

What Is This Thing Called Love?
Charles B. Cochran's London revue *Wake Up and Dream* was brought
to Broadway by Arch Selwyn. Songs by Cole Porter included this
popular number that became one of the hits of the show. Its
interesting melodic nuances with changes from major to minor modes
made it a favorite of jazz players, and it has since become an enduring
standard. (1929)

You've Got That Thing
Fifty Million Frenchmen is subtitled "A Musical Tour of Paris," and Paris
was a place well-known to Cole Porter. The show was a big success
with its other scintillating songs "Find Me a Primitive Man" and "You
Do Something to Me." (1929)

Love For Sale
Cole Porter's sophisticated song from *The New Yorkers* raised a few
eyebrows at its unabashed lyrics dealing with prostitution. Kathryn
Crawford and three girl friends (June Shafer, Ida Pearson, and Stella
Friend) introduced it in the show. Cover art is appropriately by Peter
Arno of *New Yorker* magazine fame. (1930)

Hit shows followed one another in rapid succession
containing unforgettable Cole Porter songs that have become
theater classics today. Refined, elegant, charming, and witty,
his sometimes unorthodox harmonies and word rhymes
never failed to enchant his audiences with their fresh
approach. Other major show successes were *The Gay
Divorce* (1932) with song "Night and Day"; *Jubilee* (1935)
with "Begin the Beguine" and "Just One of Those Things";
and *Can-Can* (1953) with "C'est Magnifique," and "I Love
Paris." Movies that featured popular Porter songs include
Born To Dance (1936) with "I've Got You Under My Skin":
Rosalie (1937) with "In the Still of the Night; *Hollywood
Canteen* (1944) with "Don't Fence Me In," and *Adam's Rib*
(1949) with "Farewell, Amanda."

More Cole Porter Show Songs

I Get a Kick Out of You
Inimitable Ethel Merman belted out this song with William Gaxton (left) in the Cole Porter musical *Anything Goes*, also featuring Victor Moore (right). Other memorable songs from the score were "All Through the Night," "Blow, Gabriel, Blow," "You're the Top," and the title song. (1934)

It's D'Lovely
The musical comedy *Red Hot and Blue* again starred vivacious Ethel Merman who sang this song with Bob Hope in the show. Other Cole Porter songs from the show include "You've Got Something" and "Ridin' High." (1936)

My Heart Belongs to Daddy
Mary Martin, swathed in furs with curvy legs exposed, sang coyly of the benefits of having a "sugar daddy" in Cole Porter's show *Leave It To Me!* establishing her as a major talent. Others in the cast were Victor Moore, Sophie Tucker, William Gaxton, and dancer Gene Kelly. (1938)

Always True to You in My Fashion
Kiss Me Kate was Cole Porter's blockbuster musical based on Shakespeare's *The Taming of the Shrew*. Lisa Kirk introduced this song in the original Broadway show that also included Alfred Drake and Patricia Morison in the fine cast. The show ran for 1,070 performances and yielded many outstanding Porter songs including "Why Can't You Behave," "So In Love," "Too Darn Hot," and "Wunderbar." (1948)

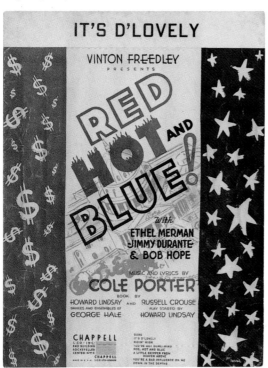

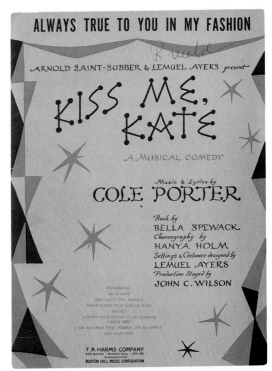

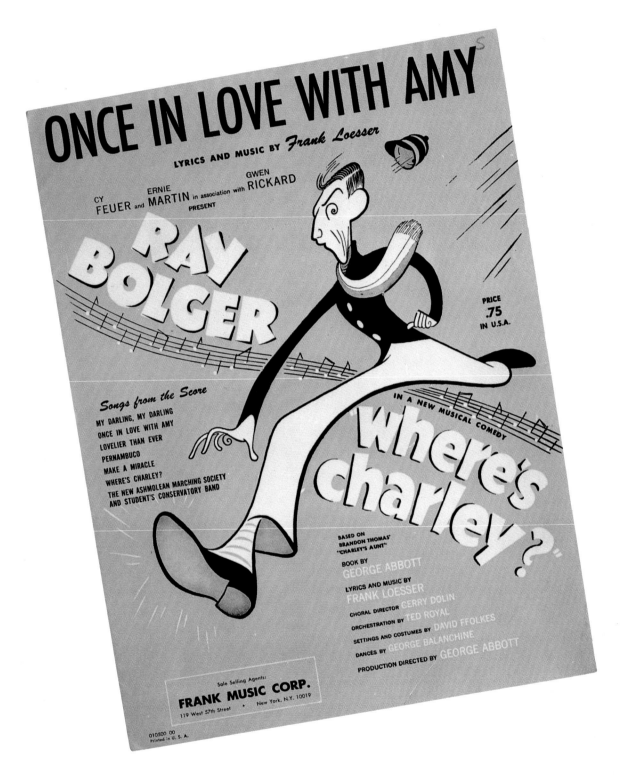

CHAPTER 4:
OTHER LUMINARIES OF THE MUSICAL THEATER

The lyricism and professionalism of Victor Herbert, the vitality and enthusiasm of George M. Cohan, and the warmth and versatility of Irving Berlin started American musical theater in a new direction in the early twentieth century. Subsequent innovations by Jerome Kern and George Gershwin, and the new sophistication of Cole Porter were carried on and energized by new songwriters. American musical comedy had come into its own, and had truly become an international art form.

Some composers wrote music over a great span of time; Irving Berlin is an example of such longevity. Other musical comedy songwriters seemed to have peak productive years during which their creative expression reflected the style of an era so perfectly that they will forever be identified with it.

Jerome Kern, George and Ira Gershwin, Vincent Youmans, and the team of B. G. DeSylva, Lew Brown, and Ray Henderson dominated the 1920s. Cole Porter, Richard Rodgers and Lorenz Hart, and Howard Dietz with Arthur Schwartz reflect the 1930s. Rodgers and Oscar Hammerstein II, Alan Lerner and Frederick Loewe, Kurt Weill, and Leonard Bernstein had their greatest impact in the 1940s and 1950s. The 1960s saw the talents of Jerry Herman, Lionel Bart, the teams of Sheldon Harnick and Jerry Bock, Mitch Leigh and Joe Darion, and John Kander and Fred Ebb. The 1970s to the present brought out the talents of Stephen Sondheim, Marvin Hamlisch, Claude-Michel Schönberg, and Andrew Lloyd Webber.

DeSylva, Brown, and Henderson Show Songs

DeSylva, Brown, and Henderson were a dynamic team of songwriters in the 1920s. Ray Henderson (1896-1970) wrote the music, and Lew Brown (1893-1958) and B. G. DeSylva (1895-1950) worked together on the lyrics. Each of the three had written hit songs with others before forming their partnership, but together they reached new heights of creativity, particularly the many hit songs written for *George White's Scandals* including "Lucky Day," "The Birth of the Blues," and "Black Bottom."

It All Depends on You
Al Jolson was a singing sensation when he introduced this DeSylva, Brown, and Henderson song in the musical show *Big Boy*. (1926)

Previous page photo:
Once In Love with Amy
Frank Loesser wrote *Where's Charley?*, a popular musical based on the farce *Charley's Aunt*, with Ray Bolger doing the female impersonation to great critical reviews. "My Darling, My Darling" was another hit song by Loesser that got the romantic treatment from handsome leading man Byron Palmer. The show had great audience appeal and ran for 792 performances. (1948)

Good News
Good News, a sparkling musical in a college setting, featured songs by DeSylva, Brown, and Henderson that went on to become hits—"The Best Things In Life Are Free," "Varsity Drag," and "Lucky In Love." This title song introduced by Zelma O'Neal reportedly stopped the show. (1927)

Button Up Your Overcoat
Follow Thru, a musical in a country club setting, followed the success of *Hold Everything!*—this time lampooning golf rather than boxing. Jack Haley and Zelma O'Neal introduced this hit song in the show followed by a sparkling tap-dance by Eleanor Powell. (1928)

You're the Cream in My Coffee
The songwriting team of DeSylva, Brown, and Henderson wrote this memorable song for *Hold Everything!*, a musical about prize-fighting. Jack Whiting and Ona Munson introduced it to an appreciative audience. Cover art of the lady boxer is by Helen Van Doorn Morgan. (1928)

Vincent Youmans' Show Songs

Vincent Youmans (1898-1946) was another stellar composer of the 1920s. He was a song plugger with Harms before joining the U.S. Navy in 1917 during World War I. His unit's bandmaster happened to be John Philip Sousa who liked Youmans' piece "Hallelujah" and featured it in Navy concerts. The song, fitted with lyrics, was later included in the Youmans' 1927 show *Hit the Deck*.

After his stint in the Navy, Youmans returned to Broadway where he wrote a number of lesser shows before hitting the big time with *No, No, Nanette* in 1925. Other shows with Youmans' music were *Oh, Please* (1926) with "I Know That You Know"; *Great Day* (1929) with "More Than You Know," "Great Day," and "Without a Song"; *Smiles* (1930) with "Time on My Hands"; and *Through the Years* (1932) with "Drums in My Heart" and "Through the Years."

Oh Me! Oh My!
Lyrics for this song from *Two Little Girls in Blue* were written by Ira Gershwin, using the pseudonym Arthur Francis (the names of his younger brother and sister). The clever plot line involved twins trying to get to India to claim a fortune, with money for only one boat ticket, so one becomes a stowaway. The show was Vincent Youmans' first major theatrical success running for 135 performances. (1921)

I Know, That You Know
This exuberant song with music by Vincent Youmans and lyrics by Anne Caldwell was performed by Canadian-born Beatrice Lillie in *Oh, Please!* Despite her dynamic presence and the antics of Charles Winninger the show was a dud, but the song lived on in the standard repertoire. (1926)

I Want to Be Happy
No No Nanette featured this outstanding song by Vincent Youmans with lyrics by Irving Caesar. It was introduced by Charles Winninger and Louise Groody in the New York production at the Globe Theatre. The well-known standard "Tea for Two" was another hit from the show. A successful revival in 1971 starred Ruby Keeler. (1924)

Sometimes I'm Happy
The musical comedy *Hit the Deck* starred Louise Groody and Charles King who introduced this snappy song with words by Leo Robin and Clifford Grey, and music by Youmans. "Hallelujah" was another hit from the show that ran for 352 performances. (1927)

Kurt Weill Show Songs

Kurt Weill (1900-1950) was a German composer, classically trained in theory and composition, who left his mark on American musical theater of the 1930s and 1940s. His *Threepenny Opera*, introduced in Germany in 1928, was a social commentary on the moral decadence in Europe. Its best-known song was "The Ballad of Mack the Knife." Though popular with the German public, the show did not find favor with the new Nazi regime, and Weill was forced to flee his country in 1933. He continued to compose in Paris and London before coming to the United States.

My Ship
Gertrude Lawrence sang this dreamy song in Weill's *Lady In the Dark*, an interesting theatrical venture with book by Moss Hart that took on the world of psychoanalysis and effectively introduced dream sequences into musical comedy. Lyrics by Ira Gershwin. (1941)

Mack the Knife
A German import from *The Threepenny Opera* has become a classic with its English words by Marc Blitzstein and memorable music by Kurt Weill. It was introduced by Lotte Lenya in the opera, and was revived with great success in the 1960s by Louis Armstrong. (1928)

In 1937 Weill applied for U. S. citizenship, and started work on *Knickerbocker Holiday* which subtly attacked dictatorship in the modern day world by drawing parallels with historical New Amsterdam. Subsequent Broadway offerings included *Lady in the Dark, One Touch of Venus, The Firebrand of Florence, Street Scene, Down in the Valley,* and *Love Life.* His last musical, *Lost In the Stars* (1949), was a tragedy dealing with racial problems with score by Weill and book by Maxwell Anderson.

Speak Low
Mary Martin and Kenny Baker introduced this seductive song in the successful musical *One Touch of Venus* with music by Weill and lyrics by Ogden Nash. Martin played a statue of Venus that comes to life in this light-hearted production. (1943)

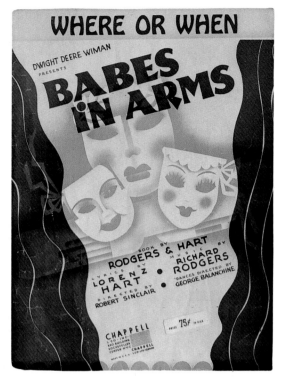

Where or When
Some of Rodgers and Hart's finest songs were featured in *Babes in Arms*, including this song introduced by Ray Heatherton and Mitzi Green. Other songs included "My Funny Valentine," "I Wish I Were in Love Again," "Johnny One Note," and "The Lady Is a Tramp." (1937)

I Married an Angel
This show was an outstanding critical success for Rodgers and Hart. It was a fantasy musical starring Dennis King with the beautiful fragile Vera Zorina from the Ballet Russe de Monte Carlo portraying the angel. Besides the title song it introduced the lovely Rodgers and Hart song "Spring Is Here." (1938)

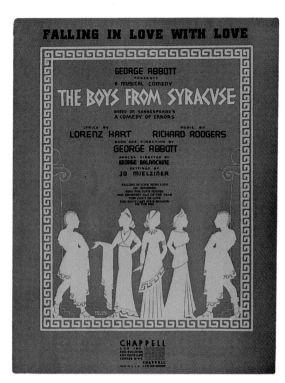

Falling in Love with Love
The Boys from Syracuse was based on Shakespeare's play *The Comedy of Errors* about two sets of twins with the same names, and the consequent hilarious mix-ups. Other inspired Rodgers and Hart songs from the show were "This Can't Be Love" and "Sing for Your Supper." It had 235 performances. (1938)

Rodgers and Hammerstein Show Songs

After Hart's death in 1943, Richard Rodgers teamed up with lyricist **Oscar Hammerstein II** (1895-1960) on the production of *Oklahoma*. This, their first collaboration, began a long and fruitful association. A perfect blend of drama, song, and dance, *Oklahoma* was a popular and critical success, and was awarded a special Pulitzer prize citation in recognition of its creative excellence. Rodgers and Hammerstein continued to write hit shows, one after the other, and their shows and songs dominated the musical theater scene until Hammerstein's death in 1960.

Rodgers also wrote the monumental score for *Victory At Sea* (1952), a documentary film of naval encounters during World War II that ran for twenty-six weeks over the NBC-TV network. This was arranged into an effective orchestral suite by Robert Russell Bennett. "Guadalcanal March" from the suite was released as sheet music in 1952. Other significant symphonic compositions by Rodgers were the aforementioned ballet music for "Slaughter on Tenth Avenue," and the "Waltz Suite" from *Carousel*.

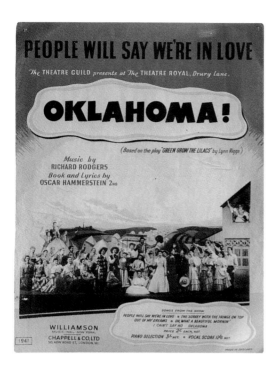

People Will Say We're in Love
Alfred Drake and Joan Roberts introduced this song in the original New York production of *Oklahoma*, a production that ran for a phenomenal 2,248 performances. The music shown here is from the Theatre Guild version presented in London in 1947 that also had a long run of 1,548 performances. Other hit songs included "Oh, What a Beautiful Mornin'," "The Surrey with the Fringe on Top," "Out of My Dreams," and the rollicking title song. (1943)

June Is Bustin' Out All Over
Rodgers and Hammerstein's *Carousel* was another big success for the team. This ebullient song, introduced by Christine Johnson, Jan Clayton, and the ensemble, was one of many hits from the show. Other memorable classics were "If I Loved You," "What's the Use of Wond'rin'," "You'll Never Walk Alone," and Richard Rodgers' acclaimed opening overture, "The Carousel Waltz." (1945)

The Gentleman Is a Dope
Allegro failed to match the success of *Oklahoma* and *Carousel* but it yielded several fine Rodgers and Hammerstein songs including "So Far," "A Fellow Needs a Girl," and this standard classic introduced by Lisa Kirk in the show. (1947)

Some Enchanted Evening
The felicitous combination of a navy nurse played by Mary Martin, and a French planter played by opera singer Ezio Pinza, and an outstanding Rodgers and Hammerstein score ensured the success of *South Pacific* which won the 1950 Pulitzer Prize for drama. Other songs included "There Is Nothin' Like a Dame," "Younger than Springtime," and "I'm Gonna Wash that Man Right Out of My Hair," sung by Mary Martin who, indeed, washed her hair on stage at each performance. (1949)

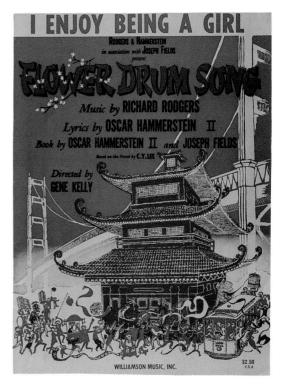

We Kiss In a Shadow
The lavish colorful production of *The King and I* was another jewel in the Rodgers and Hammerstein crown of successes. The original cast included Yul Brynner as the Siamese king and Gertrude Lawrence as the schoolteacher Anna. This song was introduced by Doretta Morrow and Larry Douglas. Other wonderful songs included "Hello, Young Lovers," "I Whistle a Happy Tune," and "Getting to Know You." (1951)

Do I Love You Because You're Beautiful?
Rodgers and Hammerstein tried their hand at writing for television with the score for *Cinderella*, a vehicle for Julie Andrews. The 1957 performance was not videotaped, and Rodgers later commented in his autobiography about the impact of television, that *Oklahoma!* took over five years to play to 4 million people, and, in contrast, the single TV performance of *Cinderella* was seen by 107 million viewers. It was later videotaped with a new script and cast. (1957)

I Enjoy Being a Girl
Flower Drum Song dealt with the cultural conflicts in an Asian family in San Francisco's Chinatown. Miyoshi Umeki portrayed the Chinese-American girl, and introduced this song in the show. Gene Kelly directed the original production that also included noteworthy songs "You Are Beautiful," "A Hundred Million Miracles," and "Love, Look Away." The show had a successful run of 600 performances. (1958)

My Favorite Things
Based on the Trapp family story of a dramatic escape from the Nazis in wartime Austria, *The Sound of Music* had a sound plot as well as a superb cast and Rodgers and Hammerstein score. This delightful song was introduced by opera singer Pat Neway playing the Mother Abbess and Mary Martin as the postulant Maria. Other songs included "Climb Ev'ry Mountain" and the title song. (1959)

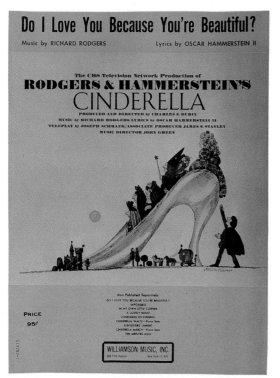

Show Songs of Grieg, Borodin, Robert Wright, and George Forrest

Song of Norway was a popular show of the 1940s with music by **Robert Wright** (born 1914) and **George Forrest** (born 1915). This songwriting team had a predilection for the music of classical composers, and two of their biggest successes were based on the lives and music of Norwegian composer Edvard Grieg and Russian composer Alexander Borodin.

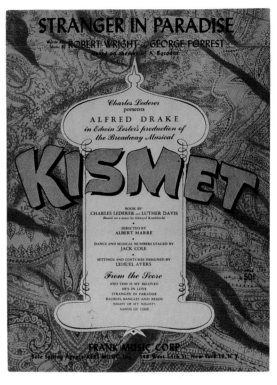

Strange Music
Song of Norway was based on the life of composer Edvard Grieg, with Grieg's music adapted by Robert Wright and George Forrest. Lawrence Brooks and Helena Bliss introduced this song in the show. The operetta was first performed by the Los Angeles Civic Light Opera Company, then moved on to New York. Audiences were well pleased with the show, particularly the Grieg melodies and the skillful choreography by George Balanchine, and it had a lengthy run of 860 performances. (1944)

Stranger in Paradise
This lovely duet was introduced by Doretta Morrow and Richard Kiley in *Kismet*. The original cast also included the incomparable Alfred Drake singing "Gesticulate," "The Olive Tree," and "Rhymes Have I." Other outstanding songs from the production were the trio "And This Is My Beloved" sung on a split stage, and the exotic songs "Baubles, Bangles, and Beads" and "Sands of Time." The Wright and Forrest score was adapted from the music of Alexander Borodin. *Kismet* had 583 performances on Broadway. (1953)

Frank Loesser Show Songs

Frank Loesser (1910-1969) was primarily a lyricist before he went into the Army during World War II. During his three year stint in the military as a private, he wrote many patriotic songs and a few Army shows which paved the way for his reentry into civilian life as a composer/lyricist. After the war he hit the big time with a string of theatrical successes. He also wrote many wonderful movie songs including "Jingle, Jangle, Jingle" (music by Joseph J. Lilley) for *Forest Rangers* (1942); "They're Either Too Young or Too Old" (music by Arthur Schwartz) for *Thank Your Lucky Stars* (1943); and "I Wish I Didn't Love You So" for *The Perils of Pauline* (1947). "Baby, It's Cold Outside" in *Neptune's Daughter* won an Oscar for best movie song of 1949.

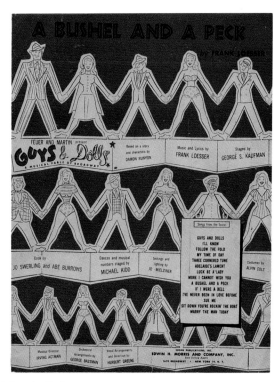

A Bushel and a Peck
Loesser had another major hit in *Guys and Dolls*, based on a story and characters by Damon Runyon. It had a raft of good songs—"I've Never Been In Love Before," "If I Were a Bell," "Luck Be a Lady," and "Adelaide's Lament"—sung by a cast that included Robert Alda, Vivian Blaine, and Sam Levene. It ran for 1,200 performances. (1950)

Gideon Briggs, I Love You
Frank Loesser's superior score for *Greenwillow* received wide acclaim for its sensitivity and poetic conception, but it failed to make a hit on Broadway. The play was based on a play by B. J. Chute, and Anthony Perkins was chosen for the lead in the musical. Other memorable songs include "Greenwillow Christmas" and "Summertime Love." (1960)

Somebody, Somewhere
Frank Loesser outdid himself with his wonderful musical play *The Most Happy Fella*. He not only composed the music, but also created his own libretto based on the play *They Knew What They Wanted* by Sidney Howard. The story of an old Italian vineyard owner and a mail-order bride inspired a Loesser score that was almost operatic in concept, highly praised by critics. Audiences knew what they wanted too, and the show ran for 676 performances in New York. (1956)

I Believe in You
Loesser won a Tony award for his integral use of lyrics to advance the plot and characters of the musical *How To Succeed In Business Without Really Trying*. The play itself won the Pulitzer Prize for drama and the Critic's Circle Award for best musical comedy of the season. The cast included Robert Morse, Charles Nelson Reilly, and Rudy Vallee. 1,417 performances. (1961)

Leonard Bernstein Show Songs

Leonard Bernstein (1918-1990) had the genius to combine the worlds of classical music and popular musical theater. He was a distinguished symphony orchestra conductor, an articulate lecturer, a gifted pianist, and a fine composer for both theater and concert hall. Bernstein's theatrical work carried on the social timeliness of Jerome Kern's *Show Boat* and Kurt Weill's *Threepenny Opera*. His shows include *On The Town* (1944), *Wonderful Town* (1952), *Candide* (1956), and his electrifying *West Side Story* (1957).

Ohio
Wonderful Town was based on the play *My Sister Eileen*. It was set in Greenwich Village in the 1930s and starred Rosalind Russell as a career girl who tries to protect her younger sister, Edie Adams, from improper male advances. Bernstein again worked with Comden and Green on a bright score including this nostalgic song. The show ran for 559 performances. (1953)

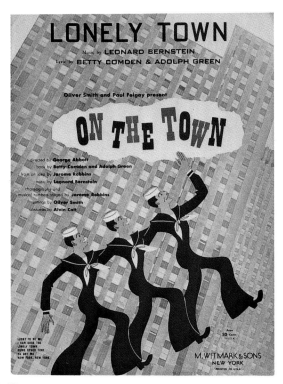

Lonely Town
Betty Comden and Adolph Green supplied the book and lyrics for *On the Town* with scintillating music by Leonard Bernstein, and outstanding choreography by Jerome Robbins. The plot line told of three sailors on shore leave in Manhattan who meet three girls in a bar. (1945)

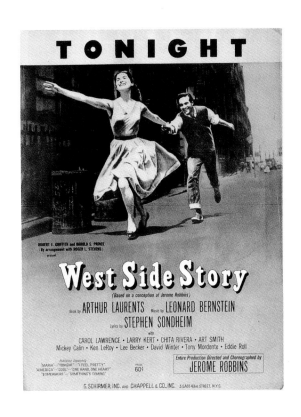

Tonight
Loosely based on the theme of *Romeo and Juliet*, *West Side Story* changed the locale to the West Side of Manhattan and the protagonists to Puerto Rican versus native-born American teenagers. The dramatic score included the lyrical beauty of "Maria" and "Tonight," and the rhythmic complexities and angular melodic lines of "America" and "Something's Coming." (1957)

Lerner and Loewe Show Songs

Lyricist **Alan Jay Lerner** (1918-1986) and composer **Frederick Loewe** (1901-1988) dazzled the musical theater with many hit shows in the mid-twentieth century. *My Fair Lady*, based on George Bernard Shaw's *Pygmalion* tale, ran for an astounding 2,717 performances with a cast including Rex Harrison and Julie Andrews. It was later made into a movie with Audrey Hepburn playing the part of Eliza Doolittle and Rex Harrison in his original Broadway role of Professor Higgins.

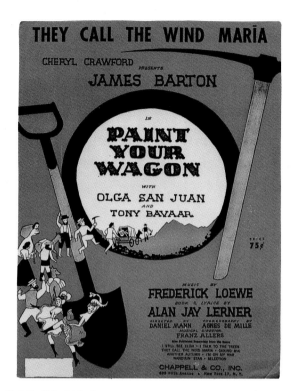

They Call the Wind Maria
Lerner and Loewe wrote songs with a Western twang for the musical production *Paint Your Wagon* starring James Barton and Olga San Juan. Other good songs from the show were "I Still See Elisa," "I Talk to the Trees," "I'm On My Way,' and "Wand'rin' Star." (1951)

Almost Like Being in Love
Brigadoon was a fantasy show enshrouded in Scottish mist that delighted audiences, and earned the first ever Drama Critics Circle Award for best musical of the year. Lerner and Loewe's enchanting songs included "The Heather on the Hill" and "I'll Go Home With Bonnie Jean," and "Come to Me, Bend to Me." (1947)

On the Street Where You Live
A little-known ingénue, Julie Andrews, captivated audiences as the cockney flower girl Eliza Doolittle in the original production of *My Fair Lady*. Other popular songs from the show were "I Could Have Danced All Night," "Wouldn't It Be Loverly," "I've Grown Accustomed to Her Face," and "Get Me to the Church On Time." Clever cover art is by Hirschfeld, whose fans find it intriguing to search for the letters "NINA" which he sometimes hid in his drawings, a tribute to his daughter. The name is part of the fringe on the lady's scarf, with Hirschfeld's name at the other end. (1956)

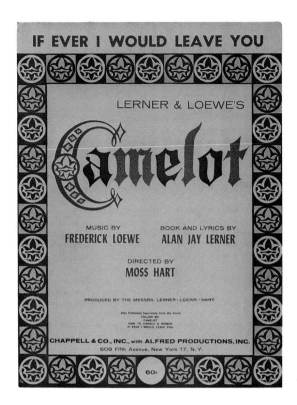

If Ever I Would Leave You
The popular show *Camelot* had an original cast that included Richard Burton as King Arthur, Robert Goulet as Lancelot, and Julie Andrews as Guinevere, almost guaranteeing its success. The score by Lerner and Loewe, the magnificent sets, and sumptuous costumes added to its glory and contributed to its lengthy run of 837 performances. (1960)

Other Memorable Broadway Shows

Hernando's Hideaway
Richard Adler (born 1921) and Jerry Ross (1926-1955) hit it big with *The Pajama Game* which ran for 1,063 performances. Newcomer Shirley MacLaine dazzled audiences with her dance performance of "Steam Heat." Other songs from the show included "I'm Not At All In Love" and "Hey, There." (1954)

Shoeless Joe from Hannibal Mo.
Richard Adler and Jerry Ross collaborated on the score for *Damn Yankees*, a musical based on the novel *The Year the Yankees Lost the Pennant* by Douglass Wallop. The Faustian legend of a man who makes a deal with the devil is told in a baseball context. Gwen Verdon dominated the show with her dancing and singing, shown here on the cover of a song from the movie version. (1955)

How Are Things in Glocca Morra?
Composer Burton Lane (born 1912) and lyricist E. Y. Harburg (1898-1981) were a hit combination with their fantasy show *Finian's Rainbow* co-starring Ella Logan, David Wayne, and Donald Richards, with the character Finian played by the Irish comedian Albert Sharpe. Lane and Harburg's other fine songs from the play were "If This Isn't Love," "Old Devil Moon," "When I'm Not Near the Girl I Love," and "Look to the Rainbow." (1946)

Seventy Six Trombones

Meredith Willson (1902-1984), composer, flautist, and conductor, worked in the concert theater, radio, and movies. Though he played with the New York Philharmonic for several years and composed two symphonies, it was in the world of popular music that he met his greatest success. *The Music Man* was a smash hit in 1957 with songs "Seventy-Six Trombones" and "Till There Was You," followed by *The Unsinkable Molly Brown* in 1960 with "I Ain't Down Yet" and "Belly Up to the Bar, Boys." (1957)

The Party's Over

Jule Styne's music in *Bells Are Ringing* was embellished with lyrics by Betty Comden and Adolph Green. Judy Holliday stole the show as an answering-service girl who gets involved with her telephone clients. The show ran for 924 performances, and was then made into a Hollywood movie starring Miss Holliday. "Just In Time" was another song hit from the show. (1956)

Papa, Won't You Dance With Me?

Jule Styne (1905-1994) wrote the music for a myriad of hit shows including *High Button Shoes*, for which Sammy Cahn wrote the lyrics. This period piece set in 1913 featured Phil Silvers' slapstick comedy and Nanette Fabray's singing and dancing. A take-off on Mack Sennett's Keystone Kops comedies resulted in a lawsuit by Mr. Sennett that was settled out of court. Played 727 performances. (1947)

Let Me Entertain You

This story was suggested by the memoirs of Gypsy Rose Lee, and centers on her domineering mother portrayed incomparably by Ethel Merman. Jule Styne's music received critical accolades as the best he had ever written, and Stephen Sondheim's lyrics struck just the right sentiment. Other songs from the score included "Some People," "Everything's Coming Up Roses," "I Had a Dream," and the finale "Rose's Turn." (1959)

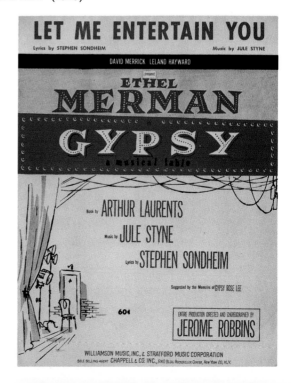

'Til Tomorrow
Fiorello starred Tom Bosley as Mayor Fiorello La Guardia in this Pulitzer Prize winning biographical production with memorable lyrics by Sheldon Harnick and a critically acclaimed score by Jerry Bock. This ballad in waltz time was one of the popular hits of the show. (1959)

Show Songs from the 1960s

The 1960s was an age of social upheaval in America. The assassination of President John F. Kennedy in November 1963 triggered an escalation of the Vietnam War, and the concomitant disagreements about United States' involvement. Rebellion by the youth of the country was seen in long hair, draft dodgers, peace-niks, flower children, and rock music.

Bright new stars shone in the musical theater firmament in the 1960s. **Lionel Bart** (b. 1930) wrote the book, music, and lyrics for the hit London production *Oliver*, that enjoyed further success when brought to America in 1963. **Jerry Herman** (born 1933) wrote the solid scores for *Hello, Dolly!* and *Mame*. Composer **Jerry Bock** (b. 1928) and lyricist **Sheldon Harnick** (b. 1924) followed their successful *Fiorello* with *Fiddler on the Roof*. Composer **Jule Styne** (1905-1994) teamed up with lyricists **Betty Comden** (b. 1919) and **Adolph Green** (b. 1915) on *Do Re Mi*, and with **Bob Merrill** on the mega-hit *Funny Girl*.

Other long-running shows of the decade were *Man Of La Mancha* (1965) by **Mitch Leigh** and **Joe Darion**; and *Cabaret* (1966) by **John Kander** and **Fred Ebb**. The first rock musical *Hair* opened on Broadway in 1968 beginning a new trend in musical theater. Also deserving mention from the 1960s are the shows:

Bye Bye Birdie (1960)—W/Lee Adams, M/Charles Strouse;
Milk and Honey (1961)—WM/Jerry Herman;
No Strings (1962)—WM/Richard Rodgers;
Stop the World-I Want to Get Off (1962)—WM/Leslie Bricusse and Anthony Newley;
Golden Boy (1964)—W/Lee Adams, M/Charles Strouse;
What Makes Sammy Run? (1964)—WM/Ervin Drake;
I Do! I Do! (1966)—W/Tom Jones, M/Harvey Schmidt.

As Long As He Needs Me
Oliver was a smash hit in London with a lengthy run of 2,618 performances before it came to the Broadway stage. It was based on Charles Dickens' *Oliver Twist* about the tribulations of a young orphan boy. Lionel Bart's score with songs "Consider Yourself," "Where Is Love," "Who Will Buy," and "I'd Do Anything" won him Tony Awards for best composer and lyricist. (1960)

Sunrise, Sunset
Broadway's longest running musical ever was *Fiddler on the Roof*, and it won just about every award available for a musical show. The colorful plot was set in a Russian-Jewish village, and included such characters as the rabbi, the matchmaker, and a dairy farmer and his wife and their marriageable daughters. Zero Mostel was perfect as Tevya, the father, and the enchanting score with lyrics by Sheldon Harnick and music by Jerry Bock guaranteed the show's success. Other songs were "If I Were a Rich Man," "Matchmaker, Matchmaker," and "Miracle of Miracles." (1964)

Hello, Dolly!
Hello, Dolly!, based on *The Matchmaker* by Thornton Wilder, starred the irrepressible Carol Channing as Dolly. Music and lyrics were written by Jerry Herman, and the show was directed and choreographed by Gower Champion. Critics and audiences alike loved the show, and it won the Critics Circle Award for best musical comedy of the season, as well as ten Tony Awards. (1963)

People
Funny Girl was based on the life of Fanny Brice, and starred newcomer Barbra Streisand in an incomparable portrayal of the legendary star that propelled her into superstardom. The show, with music and lyrics by Jule Styne and Bob Merrill, enjoyed a Broadway run of 1,348 performances. This song cover is from the successful movie version. (1964)

I Really Like Him
Man of La Mancha was one of Broadway's longest running shows with 2,329 performances. This romantic musical with music by Mitch Leigh and lyrics by Joe Darion featured other hit songs "The Impossible Dream" and "Dulcinea" sung by Richard Kiley as Don Quixote. (1965)

If He Walked Into My Life
Angela Lansbury **was** *Mame* in the original production of the hit show, acting the part with such vigor that she reportedly sometimes passed out in her dressing room during intermissions. She was aided and abetted by Beatrice Arthur playing an acid-tongued Vera Charles, and Frankie Michaels as young Patrick—all three of whom won Tony Awards for their efforts. (1966)

I'll Never Fall in Love Again
Neil Simon wrote the book for the musical comedy *Promises, Promises,* based on the motion picture *The Apartment.* With music by Burt Bacharach (born 1928) and lyrics by Hal David (born 1921), it enjoyed 1,281 performances on Broadway. This song enjoyed considerable popularity in the early 1960s. (1968)

Show Songs from the 1970s

Familiar names from the 1960s also made it big in the 1970s. **Stephen Sondheim** (b. 1930) entered the theater with an intense musical background from Princeton, and started out by writing incidental music for plays, and lyrics for the Broadway shows *West Side Story* and *Gypsy.* His first big success as a composer/lyricist was *A Funny Thing Happened On the Way To the Forum* (1962). Later Sondheim shows followed: *Company* (1970), *Follies* (1971), *A Little Night Music* (1973), *Pacific Overtures* (1976), *Sweeney Todd* (1979), *Merrily We Roll Along* (1981), *Sunday In the Park with George* (1984), and *Into the Woods* (1987).

Aquarius
The late sixties introduced *Hair,* described as "The American Tribal Love-Rock Musical." It met with mixed reviews, but ticket and record sales were brisk, and the show lasted for 1,742 performances, attributed by some to its hippie plot and public display of nudity. (1967)

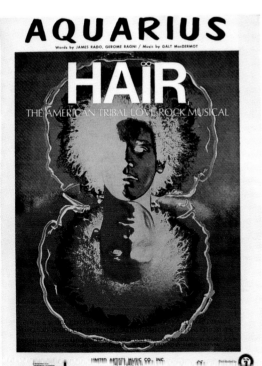

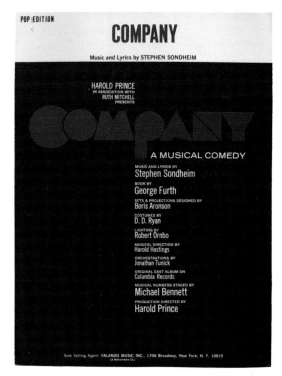

Company
Company included a score by Stephen Sondheim that reached new heights of modernity in form and harmony with interesting meter changes that gave the music an enchanting freshness. With its book by George Furth, musical numbers choreographed by Michael Bennett, all under the direction of Harold Prince, it was well received and ran for 690 performances. (1970)

Send In the Clowns
A Little Night Music was a romantic musical with wonderful Sondheim songs. It was suggested by the Ingmar Bergman movie *Smiles of a Summer Night*. Starring Glynis Johns, Len Cariou, and Hermione Gingold, it was very successful running for 600 performances. Sondheim's music won both the Critics Circle and Tony awards as best score of the season. (1973)

Charles Strouse (b. 1928) was a 1947 graduate of the prestigious Eastman School of Music in Rochester, New York, and continued his musical studies with Aaron Copland and Nadia Boulanger. He began his songwriting collaboration with lyricist Lee Adams (born 1924) in 1950. Hit musicals by the two include *Bye Bye, Birdie* (1960) and *Golden Boy* (1964). *Applause* (1970) had a great book by Betty Comden and Adolph Green based on the successful 1950 movie *All About Eve* from a story by Mary Orr. It was a big hit, running for 896 performances.

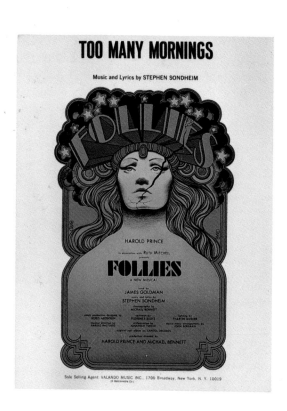

Too Many Mornings
Follies was a grandiose production, costing $800,000 to produce, but it was an immediate success and ran for a year with 521 performances. Some of its charm was in its cast which included familiar faces from the past—Ethel Shutta, Yvonne de Carlo, Alexis Smith, Gene Nelson, Fifi d'Orsay, and Dorothy Collins—portraying aging stage stars who mourn the demise of the stage musical. Sondheim's music won the Tony Award that season for best score. (1971)

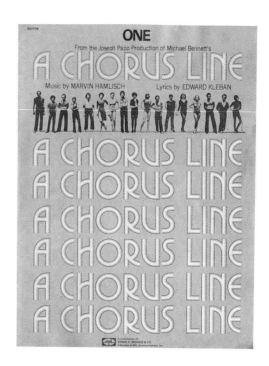

Applause
The dynamite score by Charles Strouse and Lee Adams ensured the success of *Applause*, a musical based on the movie *All About Eve*. The perfect choice of a leading lady was frosting on the cake. Lauren Bacall played the middle-aged actress Margo Channing, and her vibrant performance won her a Tony Award for best actress in a musical. Additional awards were for best director, choreographer, and best musical of the season. (1970)

One
Marvin Hamlisch wrote the music, and Edward Kleban, the words, for *A Chorus Line*, a sensitive show with a simple story line about 28 chorus dancers auditioning on a bare stage who pour out their hearts to the director. It won many awards—Pulitzer Prize for best drama of 1975-76, Critics Circle Award as best musical, and nine Tony Awards including one for the best score. "What I Did for Love" was another hit song from the show. (1975)

New Songwriters on the Horizon

Marvin Hamlisch (b. 1944), composer, pianist, and conductor, received his first major recognition with an Academy Award in 1974 for his film scores for *The Way We Were* and *The Sting* (based on music by Scott Joplin). In 1975 he wrote the score for the musical show *A Chorus Line* with lyrics by Edward Kleban (1939-1987). It was a spectacular success, and received a Tony Award for its music. He followed this in 1979 with the score for *They're Playing Our Song* with lyrics by Carole Bayer Sager.

The musical production of the Victor Hugo novel *Les Misérables*, first staged in Paris in 1980, has since swept the world, culminating in a legendary concert at the Royal Albert Hall in 1995 celebrating a ten year run in London. A parade of international singers who had portrayed the leading character Jean Valjean in countries all over the world brought the concert to a glorious end. The extraordinary score by **Claude-Michel Schönberg** with libretto by **Alain Boublil** and lyrics by **Herbert Kretzmer** stretched the world of musical theater to an almost operatic expression with three hours of music and no dialog. A later score by Schönberg for *Miss Saigon* in 1989 similarly used operatic conventions in a musical with equal success.

La Cage aux Folles
La Cage Aux Folles with a score by Jerry Herman tackled the sensitive theme of homosexuality for the first time in Broadway musical theater. It was a riotous comedy with good songs and a glamorous chorus line of men dressed in drag, and became an instant hit—Herman's first since *Mame* in 1966. (1983)

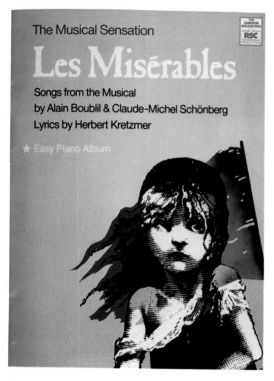

Les Misérables
The tragic Victor Hugo story of prison parolee Jean Valjean who is relentlessly stalked by police chief Javert is brought to the musical stage in the epic production *Les Misérables*. Memorable songs include the raucous humor of "Master of the House," the stirring march "Do You Hear the People Sing," the sorrowful "Empty Chairs at Empty Tables," and the exquisite prayer "Bring Him Home." (1980)

Another point of view was presented with the production of *La Cage aux Folles* in 1983. It was based on a novel by Jean Poiret, and took up the subject of homosexuality. The story tells of the relationship between two homosexuals who pretend they're straight for appearances sake. The subject was handled with delicacy and humor, and the addition of a sparkling **Jerry Herman** score delighted audiences.

In the 1970s the rock movement in theater was taken up by two young Englishmen, **Andrew Lloyd Webber** (b. 1948) and **Tim Rice** (b. 1944) who wrote the score for the rock-opera *Jesus Christ Superstar* that opened on Broadway in 1971. Despite generally negative critical reviews as to content and music, and condemnation by some religious groups, the public was curious, and the show did well, playing for 711 performances. Lloyd Webber was voted the most promising composer of the season after the New York success, and the play went to London the following year where it did even better in a lengthy run of 3,358 performances.

Lloyd Webber wrote the imaginative dance musical *Cats* in 1981 with words by Trevor Nunn, inspired by T. S. Eliot's book of children's verse, *Old Possum's Book of Practical Cats*. It was a popular long-running show in both London and New York. The score, composed in a modern vein with interesting chord changes and rhythmic variety, only yielded one popular hit song, "Memory." *Cats* was followed by such shows as *Song and Dance* (1982), *Starlight Express* (1984), and *Phantom of the Opera* (1986) that established Andrew Lloyd Webber as a new force in contemporary musical theater and earned for him the award of knighthood in 1992 for his services to the arts.

Don't Cry for Me, Argentina
The musical play *Evita* was based on the life of the glamorous Eva Peron, the tempestuous wife of Argentina's leader President Juan Peron. This popular song was introduced by Julie Covington in the original London production, and by Patti Lupone in the 1979 New York version. The show won seven Tony awards and a Grammy award for the cast album. (1976)

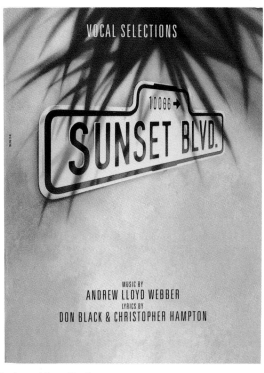

Sunset Boulevard Song Book
Another hit musical by Andrew Lloyd Webber surfaced in 1993 with lyrics by Don Black and Christopher Hampton. Based on the 1950 motion picture *Sunset Boulevard* about a fading film star, Norma Desmond, it benefited from its spectacular staging including a body floating in a swimming pool, a majestic Hollywood mansion, and split-level sets. Songs included "With One Look," "As If We Never Said Goodbye," and the title song cast in a refreshing 5/8 meter that imparted a note of appropriate agitation. (1993)

The Phantom of the Opera Song Book
The Phantom of the Opera was an instant success when it opened in London in 1982 in Her Majesty's Theater where it is still playing to capacity audiences. It opened in New York in 1985, and subsequently won seven Tony awards. The story was enhanced by the dramatic staging and special effects, and sublime music including the Phantom's plaintive "Music of the Night," the elaborately costumed "Masquerade," the poignant "Think of Me," and the haunting refrain of the title song. (1986)

THE NEWEST POPULAR WALTZ-SONG CRAZE

LET'S GO IN TO A PICTURE SHOW

WORDS BY
JUNIE McCREE

MUSIC BY
ALBERT VON TILZER

THE YORK MUSIC Co
ALBERT VON TILZER, Mg'r.
1367-9 BROADWAY, N.Y.

6

PART TWO

SILENTS, PLEASE

Opposite page:
Let's Go In to a Picture Show
Many songs were written about the new cinematic novelty, "the flickers," seen at the neighborhood picture show. This waltz song speaks of the wonders within and the funny sights on the screen. No less important was the dimness of the theater which afforded a girl and her beau an opportunity to spoon. (1909)

Chapter 5:
Silent Movie Music

Famous inventor Thomas Alva Edison pioneered the making of motion picture films in America at The Kinetographic Theater in West Orange, New Jersey, in 1893. Better known as The Black Maria, this early tar paper studio was so named because it was painted black both inside and out. It rested on a revolving base that followed the sun, thereby maximizing the time that filming could be done.

Realizing the commercial potential of his new invention, Edison arranged a public showing in New York City in 1896, at which he unveiled the Edison Vitascope in a program of projected films accompanying a vaudeville show. This show marked the beginning of a brand new art form in America that would eventually captivate the entire world--the motion picture.

Early moving pictures were curiosities, but they were here to stay. Audiences filled the theaters to view such cinematic enticements as the long kiss by vaudeville and stage stars May Irwin and John C. Rice in 1896, the championship fight between James J. "Gentleman Jim" Corbett and Robert Fitzsimmons in 1897, a demonstration by strong man Eugene Sandow strutting his stuff on film, or an action shot of the locomotive Empire State Express relentlessly bearing down on them.

In 1903 the appearance of *The Great Train Robbery* demonstrated the story telling capability of moving pictures. Produced by Edwin S. Porter, a protégé of Edison's, this landmark Western melodrama was the first movie with a plot, climaxing with actor George Barnes firing his gun into the horrified faces of the theater spectators.

Porter's production was the featured attraction in the first full-fledged motion picture theater that opened in McKeesport, Pennsylvania, in 1905. The theater was publicized as a nickelodeon because of the low admission price of five cents, and the show ran continuously from 8 a.m. to midnight. By 1908 an estimated ten million Americans were going to the picture shows, and the new industry was recognized as a lucrative venture. Moving pictures were on their way to becoming, as screenwriter Budd Schulberg remarked, "the art form of the poor."

Since Mother Goes to Movie Shows
The social impact of the movies on home life was exaggerated in this comic song. The baby is bawling, the washing, ironing, and cooking are neglected, the kitchen is a disgrace, and Fido's full of fleas—all because Mother is hardly ever home since she started going to the movies. (1916)

Take Your Girlie to the Movies
In just a few short years, the store-front nickelodeon matured into a decent theater with a large screen, a curtained stage, and comfortable seating. Young swains were well aware of the possibilities of wooing their sweeties in the dimness of a darkened movie theater, as expressed in this song. (1919)

At the Moving Picture Ball
Big-time movie makers attended this make-believe moving picture ball. Mister Zukor, Mister Thomas Ince, William Fox, and Jessie Lasky joined in the fun, and "great big stars paraded 'round the hall"—handsome Wallace Reid, Theda Bara, Alice Brady, Douglas Fairbanks, Mary Pickford, Charlie Chaplin, Blanche Sweet, and Sennett's bathing girls. The tongue-in-cheek musical directions suggest that the chorus is to be sung "Without a flicker." (1920)

Early "flickers" or "movies," as the new phenomenon was dubbed, became enormously popular. Within four years, at least eight thousand nickelodeons stretched from one end of the United States to the other. The nickelodeon was often a "Mom and Pop" business run out of a remodeled empty store with windows painted black to darken the room and to keep people from looking in. It cost a nickel to sit on folding chairs to watch the flickering figures projected on a bed sheet hung on the wall. The whole operation was primitive, and members of the family took tickets, ran the projector, and hawked popcorn, peanuts, and candy up and down the aisles. Indicative of the early informality were illuminated signs reminding the patrons of proper deportment at the show—"Please Read the Titles to Yourself. Loud Reading Annoys Your Neighbors," and the more severe remonstration "You Would Not Spit On The Floor At Home. Do Not Do It Here."

The concept of silent movie music is a curious contradiction, but from the very beginning some type of musical accompaniment was found to enhance the pantomime on the silent screen. It heightened tension, stimulated emotions, and generally contributed to a more polished product. Pianos or organs supplied background music for the action on the screen, and also helped cover the loud whirring noise of the early primitive movie projection machines. Before long the need was seen for more customized music accompaniment.

Sam Fox, a Cleveland music publisher, aware of the need for appropriate mood music to accompany silent movies, began printing a series of movie music books scored for piano in 1913. He engaged the distinguished classical violinist and composer J. S. Zamecnik to write the music for these books. Volume I in the series contained complete little pieces for different situations—funeral music, death music, war music, cowboy music, *misterioso* burglar music, clown or grotesque music, hurry-up music, and plaintive music were some of the offerings.

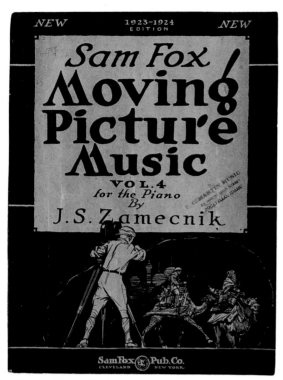

Sam Fox Moving Picture Music
Any of the books from the "Sam Fox Moving Picture Music" series are happy finds for the silent movie sheet music collector. Volume 4 has new interesting accompaniments for Canadian Mounted Police, a Chinatown den, a hunting scene, a tropic isle, and many more. (1923)

Album of Photo-Play Music
John Bunny, cover star on this folio of silent movie music, was an early comedian in Vitagraph pictures, capitalizing on his immense size (300 pounds) and clever pantomime to entertain and amuse appreciative audiences. G. Martaine compiled this album of character pieces arranged in such a way that they could be repeated as often as desired. (1914)

In a similar vein G. Schirmer published *Motion Picture Moods for Pianists and Organists* in 1924, a large thumb-indexed volume compiled by composer Erno Rapée. Rapée explains in the foreword that he tried to create a necessary bridge between the screen and the audience by making available a collection of musical pieces to fit any of fifty-two moods, from action scenes and psychological situations to simple background music designed to create atmosphere.

The book was republished in 1974, and is an interesting collection of silent screen music selected from many sources with the preponderance from classical composers. It is thoughtfully organized to maximize the pianist's fluency in making smooth transitions from one scene to the next. The music became an integral part of motion picture presentation, and was considered a vital adjunct to silent screen action.

In many cases film scores and cue sheets were written for a specific movie. Though most of these are now in libraries and museums, a few still appear occasionally at auctions. A cue sheet for the 1926 Paramount movie *Moana of the South Seas* is an interesting example of such incidental silent movie music. *Moana* would be called a documentary today, and though it was a box-office dud when first released, it is still revered for its exquisite photography of Polynesian tribal life. Filmed on location in the South Seas by Robert Flaherty, it was enhanced by complementary music that added to its exotic atmosphere and highlighted the authentic native dances in the film.

Mickey, pretty Mickey,
with your hair of raven hue..."

"Mickey," a well known theme song used to promote the silent movie of the same name, was a big seller in the sheet music market. The 1918 movie starred Mabel Normand and Lew Cody under the direction of Mack Sennett. The music was written by ragtime songwriter Charles N. Daniels under the pseudonym Neil Moret in collaboration with lyricist Harry Williams. The song was phenomenally successful, and was published with several different covers. Its success as a promotional device encouraged the further use of movie theme songs. Most of these songs in silent movie days had the same title as the movie in order to attract movie-goers. Others showed enough similarity to the film's title that they were effectively used for publicity.

Moana Cue Sheet
The *Moana* cue sheet is several pages long, consisting of 36 excerpts compiled by James C. Bradford, some composed by Bradford, others taken from classical works. Each segment is matched to a screen title, and is timed to coordinate with the action on the screen. All excerpts are in a single staff treble clef, with harmonizations left to the discretion of the accompanist. (1926)

Mickey #1
This large size printing by Daniels and Wilson, published in San Francisco, is the probable first edition. Photo of Mabel Normand in a lacy bodice, wearing a beribboned bonnet over long corkscrew curls is by Hartsook. Cover art is by LeMorgan in brown and cream tones. An alternate printing by Daniels and Wilson has different photos of Normand by Evans in Los Angeles. (1918)

Theme songs from current movies with cover photos of favorite film players further publicized the films, increased attendance, and also increased the sales of the music. These songs were played as accompaniment to the movies by pit musicians in the theaters, and were readily available to buy and play at home. Often the music was dedicated to the star, and both theme songs and dedications are a fruitful collecting area. With increasing appetite the public attended the moving picture shows, and bought and played the sheet music.

Mickey #2
The song was acquired later by Waterson, Berlin & Snyder Company who published this brown and white standard size edition with a photo by Evans. A similar cover was printed in a small format green version on a Barbelle designed background. (1918)

The star system started shortly after silent movies became popular with the public. Audiences wanted to know more about the actors and actresses who were so real to them at the picture show. Fan clubs were started, and movie magazines were published with features about the stars—their homes, their life styles, and their lovers. Many a young lady had a crush on a favorite star as evidenced by the popularity of the song "The Moving Picture Hero of My Heart."

Sheet music from the silent era spanned the years from the earliest motion pictures to the late 1920s when sound features took over. These songs are historically significant as a record of the various early film companies, independent producers, corporate mergers, featured players, and the movies themselves, of which in many cases there are no longer any surviving prints. Unfortunately a vast number of silent movies failed to survive the rigors of time. Aging film disintegrates, and little thought was given to its preservation. Some prints, thought to be useless and outdated, were deliberately destroyed, and many more were lost in studio disasters like the fire in 1937 that destroyed all the early Fox films.

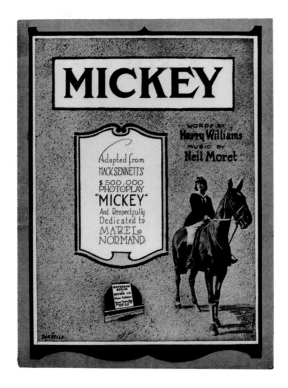

Mickey #3
This standard size version also published by Waterson, Berlin & Snyder Company, shows Miss Normand in a riding habit astride a horse. (1919)

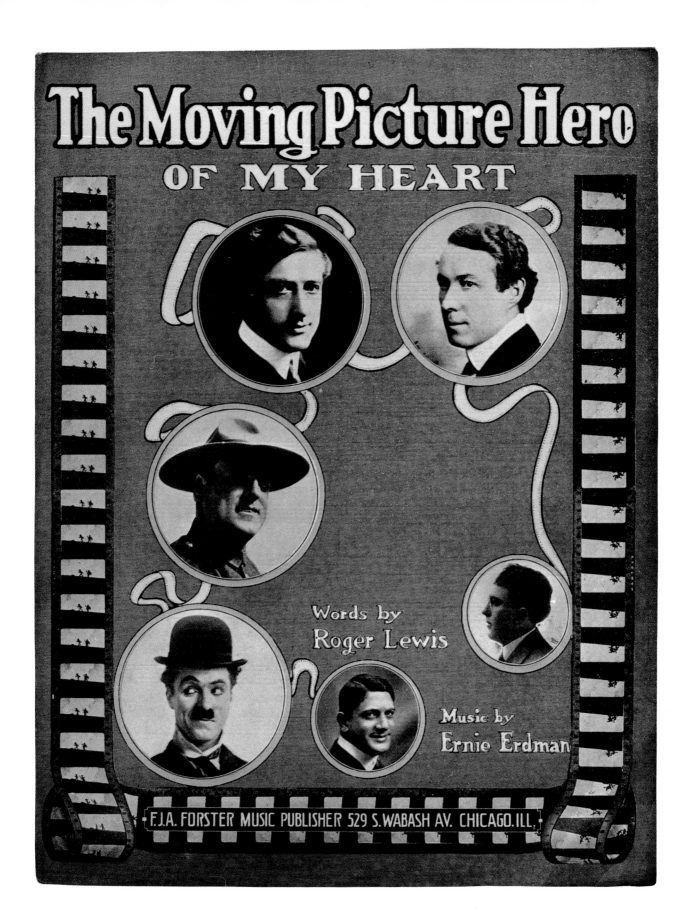

The Moving Picture Hero of My Heart
Four popular male stars of silent movies are pictured on the cover. Clockwise from bottom left are Charlie Chaplin, Broncho Billy Anderson, Francis X. Bushman, and Henry B. Walthall. The smaller circles contain pictures of the songwriters Lewis and Erdman. (1916)

CHAPTER 6:
EARLY MOVIE COMPANIES

Early film pioneers came to Hollywood from the East to escape the legal wrangling and tyranny of the Motion Picture Patents Company who sought to monopolize the budding new movie business. One of the first studios to arrive in the Los Angeles area was the American Biograph Company in 1906, soon followed by the Selig Polyscope Company from Chicago in 1907. Nestor was the first studio established in Hollywood itself in 1911, but within a year it became Universal Film Manufacturing Company, and later Universal Studios.

Other budding film companies also formed and re-formed in a constant metamorphosis. Famous Players-Lasky eventually became Paramount. Sam Goldfish and Edgar Selwyn formed Goldwyn Pictures Corporation in 1917, later merging with the Metro Picture Corporation and Louis B. Mayer Pictures into the conglomerate Metro-Goldwyn-Mayer in 1924. Mutual Film Corporation became FBO (Film Booking Offices of America), eventually becoming RKO. Vitagraph was bought by Warner Brothers in 1925. The list goes on and on. The following companies are most commonly named on silent sheet music:

American Biograph Company
Artcraft
Charlie Chaplin
DeMille Pictures Corporation
Essanay Film Manufacturing Company
Famous Players-Lasky
First National
Fox Film Corporation
Goldwyn Picture Corporation
D. W. Griffith
IMP (Independent Motion Picture Company)
Thomas H. Ince Studios
Kalem
Lubin Company
Lumière
Metro Picture Corporation
Louis B. Mayer
Mutual Film Corporation
Nestor Film Company

Paramount Pictures Corporation
Pathé
Reliance Motion Picture Company
Select Pictures Corporation
Selig Polyscope Company
Selznick Pictures
Mack Sennett
Thanhouser Company
Triangle Film Corporation
United Artists
Universal Jewel
Vitagraph
Warner Brothers
World Film Corporation

Silent Movie Innovators

D. W. Griffith

D. W. Griffith (1875-1948) was an early titan of the cinema, a directorial genius who treated the motion picture as an art form. He started out at Biograph Studio in New York writing and acting, and eventually directing and producing. His first picture was *The Adventures of Dolly*, directed for Biograph in 1908. In Hollywood in 1912 he established his reputation as a sensitive artist. Two of his early successes were *The New York Hat* and *The Mender of the Nets* featuring an engaging young actress known simply as Little Mary, eventually revealed to be Mary Pickford.

Griffith's 1915 masterpiece, *The Birth of a Nation*, was a Civil War epic that was both an artistic and financial success. The film was based on the controversial Thomas Dixon novel, *The Klansman*, and was thought by many to have racist overtones. Griffith was the son of a Confederate colonel, and brought a sympathetic Southern bias to the film for which he was criticized. The movie enflamed passions in the South, and was even blamed for some lynching episodes.

an epic production in which he told four stories simultaneously with the common theme of man's inhumanity to man, and the premise that hatred and intolerance caused all the misery in the world. The unifying factor of this unwieldy premise was a shot of Lillian Gish rocking a cradle, with Walt Whitman's words above, "Out of the cradle, endlessly rocking, Uniter of here and hereafter."

The Perfect Song
The theme song for *The Birth of a Nation* has a cover sketch of **Lillian Gish** and **Henry B. Walthall**, and is a highly prized collector's piece. Henry B. Walthall (1878-1936) was a superb stage actor with expressive eyes, and a restraint and sensitivity not usually found in actors of the silent period. His performance as the Little Colonel was lauded by critics, and he continued a successful acting career well into the sound era. (1915)

At the Fall of Babylon
Griffith's monumental production *Intolerance* was released in 1916 and though its visionary spectacle was admired, it was not successful. The Babylonian section of the movie, *The Fall of Babylon*, met with more success when it was released later as a separate feature with young **Constance Talmadge** playing the spirited Mountain Girl. Both Griffith and Miss Talmadge are seen here on the music cover that also has a fine photo of the mammoth *Intolerance* set. (1919) *Collection of Harold Jacobs*

In *The Birth of a Nation* Griffith pioneered movie-making techniques and creative editing using flashbacks, fade-outs, close-ups, and distant panoramic shots, many of which are used to this day. Additionally the production was colored with an arresting artistic quality through its use of atmospheric lighting, poetic sub-titles, and rich symbolism that took the motion picture well beyond the primitive ten minute nickelodeon flickers.

Griffith knew the importance of music in cinema. He believed that appropriate music colored the emotional tone and set the mood for a motion picture, and he engaged Joseph Carl Briel to compose a special musical score to accompany *The Birth of a Nation* using selections from classical composers. It was the first film to have its own orchestral theme, and the concept, rather like a Wagnerian operatic leitmotif, started a new trend in music that was identified with a specific movie.

Following the sensational success of *The Birth of a Nation*, Griffith embarked on his production of *Intolerance*,

Hearts of the World was Griffith's World War I triumph, a poignant drama laid in a small French village overrun by the Germans during World War I. To get background for the film, Griffith toured the trenches in Europe in 1917 finding what he termed "the aching desolation of nothingness" and "soldiers standing up to their hips in ice cold mud." He shot some footage in France of actual battle scenes, and on the Salisbury plain in the south of England, but ended up shooting most of the film in America.

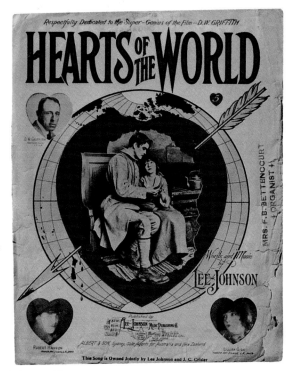

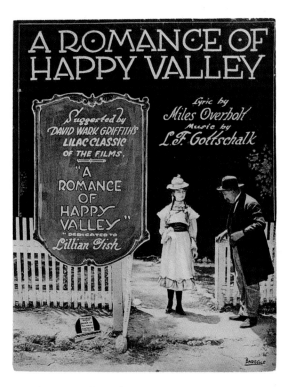

Hearts of the World
The British War Office underwrote expenses for *Hearts of the World*, and also escorted the Griffith filming party on tours of the front. Griffith's combination of documentary footage from France and fictional studio material shot in California captured the realism of war and its horrors. This theme song cover features a bleeding heart superimposed on a globe with photos of the leading stars, **Robert Harron** and **Lillian Gish**. The song was dedicated to D. W. Griffith. (1918)

A Romance of Happy Valley
Lillian Gish and **Robert Harron** played the young lovers in *A Romance of Happy Valley*, a change of pace from the heavy realism of *Hearts of the World*. The bucolic story, set in Kentucky, tells of a young man who changes his fortunes when he invents a mechanical frog and manages to sell it for $10,000. Seen with Miss Gish on the cover is **George Nichols** who played her father in the film. (1918) *Collection of Harold Jacobs*

Broken Blossoms
Lillian Gish, widely recognized as "The First Lady of the Silent Screen," starred in many outstanding Griffith films. She was one of his staunchest admirers, and he reciprocated by starring her in many of his finest movies. In *Broken Blossoms*, she portrayed the tragically abused daughter of evil Donald Crisp. This large-size song cover shows Miss Gish with **Richard Barthelmess** as the Asian man who befriends her. (1919)

Griffith subsequently left his innovative mark on a number of other studios, affiliated at one time or another with Reliance-Majestic, Triangle Corporation, Artcraft, First National, and Famous Players-Lasky before finally joining Douglas Fairbanks, Mary Pickford, and Charles Chaplin in forming the United Artists Corporation in 1919.

In 1924 Griffith stated his position on sound in motion pictures, "We do not want now and we never shall want the human voice with our films. Music—fine music—will always be the voice of the silent drama." His view was that silent film and music were a universal language, and the addition of English dialogue would alienate 95% of the world audience. His stubborn stance left him on the outside looking in when sound took over the movies in the late 1920s, and silent films were relegated to the trash heap.

Mr. Griffith was honored somewhat belatedly in 1935 with a special citation during the eighth annual Academy Award ceremonies. He was recognized "for his distinguished creative achievements as director and producer and his invaluable initiative and lasting contributions to the progress of the motion picture arts."

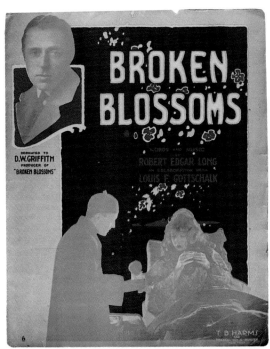

The Greatest Question
The Greatest Question, filmed under the auspices of First National studios, dealt with the psychic subject of survival after death, and is not considered Griffith at his best. Griffith again used his dependable leads, **Lillian Gish** and **Robert Harron**, who are seen here on the cover of the movie theme song. (1919) *Collection of Harold Jacobs*

Chatter-Box
Way Down East again co-starred **Lillian Gish** and **Richard Barthelmess**. Miss Gish portrayed a sweet young thing who is seduced into a sham marriage, mothers an illegitimate child who dies, and starts life in a new town. When her secret is revealed she is cast out into the snow, and the famous climax of the movie shows her in mortal danger when she is trapped on an ice-floe about to go over the falls. Griffith's long-time cameraman Billy Bitzer was praised for his brilliant photography. Character actress **Vivia Ogden**, who played the gossipy chatter-box in the movie, appears on the cover. (1920) *Collection of Harold Jacobs*

Rainbow Isle
Mr. Griffith, feeling the chill of winter descending on New York, moved his company to Florida to film *The Idol Dancer*. **Richard Barthelmess** played a derelict gin-drinking beachcomber, and **Clarine Seymour**, an idol-worshiping native dancer named White Almond Flower. During the filming Griffith embarked on a short pleasure cruise aboard the yacht *The Grey Duck*, and after an unexpected storm, was missing at sea for three days before the Navy found the party in a sheltered cove at Whale Key. Despite the attendant hoopla, Barthelmess insisted to the end that it was in no way a publicity stunt for the movie. (1920) *Collection of Harold Jacobs*

Chevalier March
Orphans of the Storm was a D. W. Griffith masterpiece starring the beautiful Gish sisters, Dorothy and Lillian, in a dramatic story set during the French Revolution. **Lillian Gish**, as Henriette, plays the protector of her blind sister, Louise, played by **Dorothy Gish**. They become parted on the streets of Paris, and endure great hardships during the storming of the Bastille. Lillian goes to the guillotine for sheltering a nobleman, but in a climactic rescue scene, is saved at the very last minute. (1922) *Collection of James Nelson Brown*

Thomas H. Ince

Thomas Ince (1882-1924) started out as a stage actor, but switched to movies around 1910. He acted in some early Biograph pictures, but was soon recruited by Carl Laemmle's IMP (Independent Motion Pictures) Company where he directed Mary Pickford in many of her IMP films of 1911. Later that year he hired the entire Miller Brothers 101 Ranch Wild West Show in California to work in his Western films to be produced under the Bison label. The Wild West troupe included a complete entourage of horses, buffalo, and authentic cowboys and Native Americans. He built a studio for filming his Westerns on 8,000 acres of land near Santa Monica that was dubbed Inceville.

Mr. Ince took the Western movie to new heights at Inceville where he made many excellent movies with Native American themes and characters, and good strong story lines. He lured his friend William S. Hart from the stage to the movies, and Hart became a popular Western star, adding to the prestige of the Ince films.

Thomas Ince was a contemporary of D. W. Griffith's, and he was also a talented and innovative director, producer, and screenwriter. He is credited with pioneering advanced production procedures and quality standards that set a model for the budding movie industry. He stuck closely to his well-structured shooting scripts, many of which he wrote himself, and insisted on authenticity of detail. Once he had approved a script it was stamped *Produce this exactly as written*, and it was an extremely detailed complete blueprint for the production.

Ince's most acclaimed and best-known work *Civilization* was released in 1915. It was a timely pacifist film with political overtones that subtly endorsed President Wilson's peace policy. The plot featured a secret organization of women united to stop war by refusing to bear any more children.

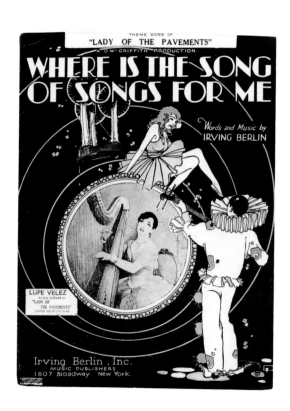

Where Is the Song of Songs for Me
Griffith experimented with sound in *Lady of the Pavements* using synchronized music, a few talking sequences, and this Irving Berlin theme song, but it was apparent that he was not comfortable with the sound medium. The movie starred **Lupe Velez** and William Boyd, but was criticized as being too heavy-handed, needing a lighter directorial touch. (1928)

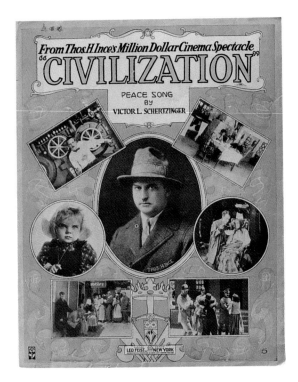

Civilization Peace Song
Handsome **Thomas Ince**'s photograph is on the cover of this theme song, flanked by six scenes from the movie *Civilization*. The pacifist lyrics pray that our country will stay away from the toils of war. A year later with the country officially at war, the song was retitled "Our Own Beloved Land," and Ince added lyrics that no longer sounded so pacifist, "...America, you have never known defeat, and now once more when forced in war, no man can dare to retreat." (1916)
Collection of James Nelson Brown

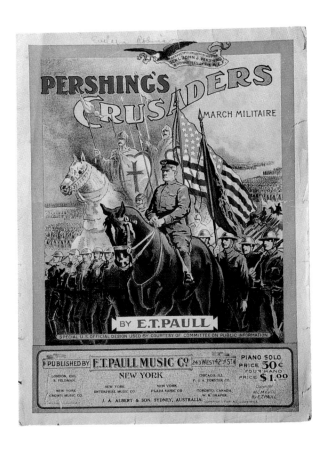

Ince died mysteriously in 1924 on a weekend party aboard William Randolph Hearst's yacht amidst rampant rumors of foul play. Death was officially attributed to heart failure, but it was whispered that Ince had been shot by a jealous Hearst who suspected him of having an affair with his protégée and mistress Marion Davies.

Thomas Ince Movie Songs

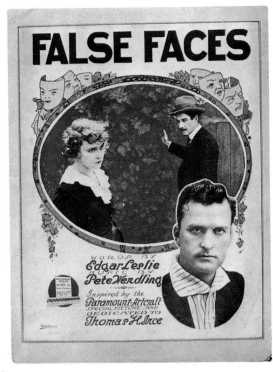

False Faces
The Paramount-Artcraft movie *False Faces* was an effective Naval spy story based on a novel by Louis Joseph Vance. This theme song cover shows the movie's co-stars **Mary Anderson** and **Henry Walthall**, and a photo of **Thomas Ince**. The "Man of a Thousand Faces," Lon Chaney, also appeared in the movie. (1919)

Pershing's Crusaders
The pro-war mood of the country was again reflected in this propaganda piece released in the early days of World War I. Newspaperman George Creel was appointed Chairman of the Committee on Public Information, a federal agency in charge of selling the war to the public. He hired **Charles S. Hart** to direct the feature-length documentary *Pershing's Crusaders*, a high quality film that was eventually seen in about a third of U. S. theaters. This E. T. Paull march has an official cover design used by courtesy of the Committee on Public Information. (1918)

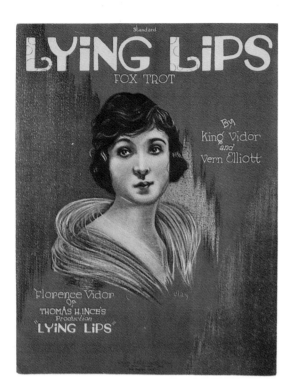

Lying Lips
This colorful art cover shows actress **Florence Vidor** who starred in the Thomas Ince film *Lying Lips* opposite **House Peters**, the handsome actor publicized as "The Star of a Thousand Emotions." Miss Vidor's then-husband **King Vidor**, who helped to write the theme song, was struggling with his own career as a director, and finally moved to the top in 1925 with his acclaimed direction of the anti-war film *The Big Parade*. (1921) *Collection of Harold Jacobs*

The Sunshine Trail
George and Ira Gershwin were induced to write this theme song to promote the Thomas H. Ince silent movie *The Sunshine Trail* starring **Douglas MacLean**. Ira used his pen name, Arthur Francis. (1923)

Lorna Doone
Madge Bellamy and **John Bowers** co-starred in the Thomas Ince production of *Lorna Doone*, a romantic, lavishly costumed adaptation of Blackmore's drama, directed by Maurice Tourneur. Miss Bellamy often portrayed innocent damsels in distress in a career that lasted from 1920 to the mid-'30s. (1922)

My Buddy
Florence Vidor and **Milton Sills** co-starred in the Thomas Ince melodrama *Skin Deep* which used this song with words by Gus Kahn and music by Walter Donaldson as its theme. Other Ince movies with published theme songs include *Peggy* (1915), *Stepping Out* (1919), *Mother O' Mine* (1921), and *Those Who Dance* (1924). (1922)

Cecil B. De Mille

Cecil B. De Mille (1881-1959) was the creative genius behind the Jesse L. Lasky Feature Play Company that came to Hollywood in 1914. The company's first production, *The Squaw Man*, was a spectacular success, and the company grew into the Paramount Picture Company, one of the giants of the motion picture industry.

De Mille brought to the silent screen some elaborate epic productions with historical and Biblical themes. Grandiose spectacles using hundreds of extras, sumptuous costumes and scenery, and intricate special effects were his specialty, and such great silent movies as *The Ten Commandments*, *The King of Kings*, and *The Sign of the Cross* endure even today. He was a tough task master who insisted on unswerving loyalty from his cast and crew, and the superior caliber of his output reflects his perfectionism. He was a strong colorful personality who strode the sets and locations in jodhpurs and high leather boots carrying a revolver, barking orders.

Cecil B. De Mille Movie Songs

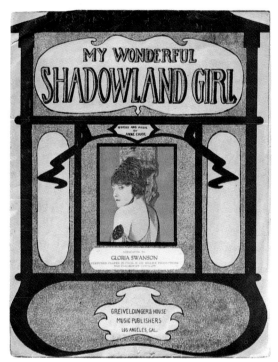

My Wonderful Shadowland Girl
Gloria Swanson, a one-time extra and slapstick comedienne in Mack Sennett shorts became a leading lady under Cecil B. De Mille's tutelage at Paramount. She rose to top stardom in a series of domestic dramas in the 1920s, and became a paragon of fashion and beauty for her admiring public. She is better remembered today as the fading silent star Norma Desmond in *Sunset Boulevard*. (1920)

Love's Old Sweet Song
In De Mille's first filming of *The Ten Commandments*, he told two stories with one theme. The prologue was the biblical story of Moses and the Tablets of Stone, and the second part told a modern day story of two brothers dealing with temptation and sin—**Richard Dix** as the good brother, and **Rod La Rocque** as the bad. The movie was a costly venture, but with its spectacular special effects like the parting of the Red Sea, it was a huge money-maker, and vindicated De Mille's spendthrift reputation. Seen on cover are Mr. Dix and leading lady **Leatrice Joy**. (1923) *Collection of Harold Jacobs*

Joan of Arc
The silent movie *Joan the Woman* was Cecil B. De Mille's first great spectacle. It starred **Geraldine Farrar**, a lovely Metropolitan Opera diva who was at the height of her career when she was summoned to Hollywood to star in silent movies. Though she sang not a note of music, she still garnered praise for her acting ability in a string of early De Mille movies. She appears here on the song cover from the epic movie. (1916)

Song of the Volga Boatmen
William Boyd was a particular favorite of producer-director Cecil B. De Mille who gave him the leading role in the silent movie *The Volga Boatman*. He is seen here on the cover of the theme song from the movie. (1926)

Heart of Humanity
The Jewel studio production *The Heart of Humanity*, directed by Allen Holubar, co-starred cover star **Dorothy Phillips** as a young war bride who wards off the advances of a sadistic Prussian soldier played by Erich von Stroheim to great critical acclaim. A famous shocking scene from the movie of von Stroheim throwing a baby out the window earned for him the name "The Man You Love to Hate." (1919)

Foolish Wives
Von Stroheim not only starred in *Foolish Wives*, but also wrote, directed, and produced it. He is seen on cover with **Miss Du Pont**, who portrayed one of the foolish wives. The film was condemned in some circles as an insult to womanhood, but such suggestions of depravity and debauchery only served to attract more business, and the movie made a tidy profit. Von Stroheim again exceeded budget, and his 320 reels were truncated to 10 in the final cutting. (1922)
Collection of Harold Jacobs

Erich von Stroheim

Erich von Stroheim (1885-1957), director and actor, was Austrian-born, the son of a Jewish hatter rather than a descendent of Austrian aristocracy as was sometimes assumed. In retrospect he is deemed one of the great directors of silent movies who took realism to shocking lengths to illustrate the depravity as well as the purity of the human situation. Because of his extravagant pursuit of accuracy in every detail and his fanatical insistence on absolute realism, he was unable to ever come within the studio's budget. His pictures were often taken away from him before completion, and given to others to finish, resulting in movies that were mere shadows of his original intentions.

Greed is considered von Stroheim's crowning success, which he brought to the screen in a stunning recreation of Frank Norris's novel *McTeague*. He completed the mammoth project with forty-two reels of film that, if left uncut, would have run for over nine hours. Studio head Irving Thalberg had it cut to two, but even in its shortened version it is a compelling drama about the lust for gold that turns men into animals.

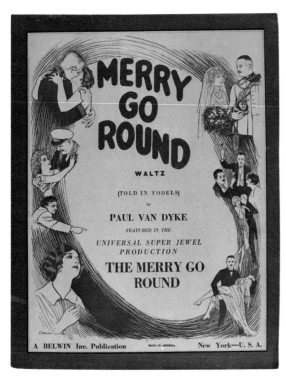

Merry Go Round
This theme song was associated with *Merry Go Round*, a dramatic silent movie set in pre-World War I Austria. Director **Erich von Stroheim** locked horns with Universal studio heads over casting, and after five weeks of shooting, again extravagantly over budget, he was replaced by director Rupert Julian. Von Stroheim's touch was said to be evident in parts of the film, due to his painstaking pre-production planning and research. (1923)

Paradise
Fay Wray appears on the cover of this theme song from *The Wedding March* co-starring **Erich von Stroheim** who also directed the film. The movie was a half-million dollars over budget, and ran for thirty-three hours before editing. It was so long that it had to be released in Europe as two movies, the second entitled *The Honeymoon*. Critics applauded the production that used music-on-disc accompaniment, Technicolor sequences, and a story of a poor girl and a prince. (1928)

I'm Laughing
The great **Erich von Stroheim** appears as *The Great Gabbo* on this music cover. Seen left to right are **Don Douglas**, **Margie Kane**, **Betty Compson**, and **von Stroheim**. This talking picture with some color sequences was directed by James Cruze. (1929)

John Ford

John Ford (1895-1973) was the younger brother of Francis Ford, an established actor/director in Hollywood serial movies. Young Jack worked his way up the ladder of success as a set laborer, propman, and occasional stuntman before turning to directing, his true forte. After turning out more than 40 movies, mostly Westerns, he directed *The Iron Horse*, one of the greatest historical spectacles yet seen on the silent screen.

The theme of the movie was the construction of the Union Pacific railroad, and Ford's cast included thousands of extras—3,000 railroad workers, 800 Pawnee, Sioux, and Cheyenne Indians, 1,000 Chinese laborers, and even a U. S. Cavalry regiment! In addition he used 2,000 horses, 10,000 Texas steer, and hundreds of buffalo. It took over a hundred cooks just to feed the cast, crew, and extras. It was a brilliant production, filmed on location in the stark Nevada desert, and it established John Ford as a director of distinction.

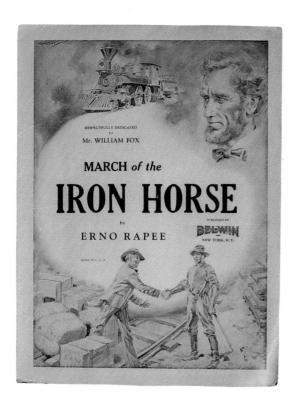

March of the Iron Horse
John Ford's direction of the monumental production *The Iron Horse* set a new standard for Western movies, unexcelled on the silent screen. The cast included George O'Brien and Madge Bellamy, but the real star was the historical recreation of the building of the Union Pacific railroad. (1924) *Collection of Jennifer Booth*

Ford's later work in sound pictures won many Academy Awards for direction—*The Informer, The Grapes of Wrath, How Green Was My Valley, The Quiet Man*, and the wartime documentaries, *The Battle of Midway* and *December 7th. The Iron Horse* would have been a front-runner for a Best Picture award in 1924, but they didn't give them out then!

John Ford's other important silent film in the 1920s was *Four Sons*, a sentimental, emotion-packed film set during World War I. Ford was beginning to gather his favorites around him, personalities that he would use over and over again in future movies. He gave a bit part to a young laborer on the Fox lot named Marion Michael Morrison (later known as John Wayne).

Vitagraph Players

Vitagraph Company, formed in 1896, was one of the early leaders in movie production whose silent movies were very popular with the public. They eventually had studios in both New York and California, and a roster of players who started with the company and became big stars later on—Maurice Costello, John Bunny, Norma Talmadge, Anita Stewart, and Rudolph Valentino, among others. Vitagraph was one of the first motion picture companies to feature actors and actresses on sheet music covers. The star system had not yet come into existence, and actors are sometimes unidentified, referred to simply as "Vitagraph Players."

Vitagraph movie covers have a certain similarity that makes them fairly easy to identify. The colors are generally in tones of sepia, brown, orange, and grey. The titles and photos are often illustrative of World War I sentiments, and were frequently published by M. Witmark & Sons.

Little Mother
The theme song of John Ford's production *Four Sons* shows **Margaret Mann** on cover rocking by her spinning wheel and dreaming of her four sons who are away at war. In this basically silent movie, Ford used occasional sound for dramatic effect. An American soldier of German origin hears a distant voice on the battlefield calling out "Mutterchen" (meaning "little mother"). In a moment of compassion, he risks his life to aid the wounded enemy soldier, only to find it is his own brother. (1928)

Maurice Costello, I Love-a Dat Man
Maurice Costello (1877-1950) was one of Vitagraph Player's stellar leading men. His most important role was Sydney Carton in the 1911 silent movie *A Tale of Two Cities*. This comic song is about a fictional Italian girl who has a crush on the famous film star. (1915)

Valse Celestia
Anita Stewart (1895-1961) starred in the silent serial *The Goddess* while working at Vitagraph. Her co-star was handsome **Earle Williams** (1880-1927), another top star at Vitagraph. The cover of this graceful waltz by Lee Orean Smith shows Miss Stewart in the title role. (1915)

The Battle Cry of Peace
Thais Lawton portrays Miss Columbia on the cover of this patriotic theme song for Vitagraph's *The Battle Cry of Peace* released on the eve of World War I. The first part of the movie showed an unarmed America being invaded by an unnamed foe. The second part showed prominent Americans propagandizing a pro-war position in subtitles said to be the longest in silent film history. (1915) *Collection of James Nelson Brown*

Your Country Needs You Now
Mary Maurice (1844-1918), seen here with **Eulalie Jensen** and **Harry Morey**, was typecast by Vitagraph as the perfect screen mother, and appears on several World War I covers including "The Little Grey Mother Who Waits All Alone," "That's a Mother's Liberty Loan," "That's All One Mother Can Do," and "The Greatest General of Them All." Mr. Morey (1873-1936) was a leading man at Vitagraph during the 'teens. (1917)

Good Bye, Little Girl Good Bye
Corinne Griffith worked for Vitagraph in New York from 1916 through 1922. She was considered one of the world's most beautiful women during the silent era, and was publicized as "The Orchid Lady." This 1904 song was reincarnated during World War I using Miss Griffith and **Walter McGrail** on the dramatic cover photograph. Mr. McGrail (1889-1970) starred in many silent movies during the 1920s, and has the dubious distinction of shared billing with wonder dog Rin Tin Tin in the 1923 Warner Brothers movie *Where the North Begins*. (circa 1917)

That Soothing Serenade
May Allison starred in movies at Metro, shown here with **Niles Welch**. Miss Allison (1895-1989) made several films from 1915 to 1927 including *A Fool There Was*. She was the wife of James Quirk, editor of *Photoplay* magazine. Mr. Welch (1888-1976) started out with Vitagraph then transferred to Metro as a leading man in the first Technicolor feature *The Gulf Between* in 1918. (1918)

Please Mr. Blacksmith Listen!
This wartime ballad tells of a child asking the village smithy to shoe his toy horse, so he can go off to war and find his big brother who is missing. Vitagraph stars **Arthur Donaldson** and **Aida Horton** pose for the scene. Small photo upper left shows Catherine Redfield who introduced this sentimental song with her Lady Bountiful Minstrels. (1918)

Your Lips Are No Man's Land but Mine
Arthur Guy Empey (1884-1963) was not really a Vitagraph contract player, but a real-life hero, a machine gunner who served in France during World War I fighting in the trenches. He suffered severe wounds in a sortie in Gommecourt Wood behind the German lines, and lived to tell about it. He took a rifle bullet in the face and two bullets in his shoulder, enduring painful operations and convalescence before his discharge. He starred in the Vitagraph film *Over the Top*, based on his famous book about his experiences at the front. Proceeds from the sale of this song were donated by Empey to the *New York Sun* Smoke Fund. (1918)

For Mary, the Baby and Me
Vitagraph stars **Agnes Ayres** and **Edward Earle** pose with a baby on the cover of this song by Paul Cunningham and James V. Monaco. Miss Ayres (1896-1940) made movies from the mid-teens through the late 1920s including a starring role opposite Rudolph Valentino in *The Sheik* in 1921. Edward Earle (1882-1972) usually played an All-American type leading man in films for both Metro and Vitagraph. (1918)

I Love You Just the Same Sweet Adeline
This song cover shows elderly stars **Jane Jennings** and **Charles Kent** at bottom. Jane Jennings was one of Vitagraph's stereotypical "mother" actresses, and Charles Kent (1852-1923) was a distinguished stage actor who worked at Vitagraph as an actor and director. Upper left shows **Agnes Ayres** with **Frank Kingsley**. (1919)

The Daughter of Rosie O'Grady
Gladys Leslie (1899-1976) of the long corkscrew curls and sparkling smile was a Vitagraph star billed by the studio as "The Girl With the Million Dollar Smile." She appeared in several silent movies from 1915 to 1925 including *Ransom's Folly* in 1915 and *Enemies of Youth* in 1925. (1918)

CHAPTER 7:
AN ALBUM OF SILENT FILM STARS

In the earliest days of Hollywood, there were no movie stars. Actors and actresses received no screen credit, and were known to audiences only by the film companies for which they worked. Many of the performers preferred such anonymity, as they were legitimate stage stars who thought it a bit degrading to appear in the new-fangled silent movies. "Picture people" were looked down on by the townspeople in Los Angeles, many of whom had posted signs on their lawns when advertising apartments for rent, "No dogs or picture people allowed."

Around 1910 Kalem began promoting its movies with theater lobby displays advertising the players, and Vitagraph had its actors and actresses making personal appearances at theaters and nickelodeons. J. Stuart Blackton, one of the founders of Vitagraph, also furthered the star policy by starting the first fan magazine in 1912, *The Motion Picture Story Magazine*, that summarized Vitagraph movie stories and displayed full page photos of Vitagraph stars to the delight of an avid public. The studio also mounted a sheet music campaign with cover photographs of its named Vitagraph Players.

By the 'teens, silent movies were so popular that favorite familiar faces at the picture show were identified. Such names as Theda Bara, Francis X. Bushman, William S. Hart, Mary Pickford, and Charlie Chaplin became household words, and the star system became firmly entrenched.

Other silent film players, less well known, contributed to the rise of motion pictures. They have remained largely unsung and many have faded into obscurity. But interest in silent movies as a lost art is gaining in strength, and as the old movies are shown at retrospectives and revivals, viewers are beginning to appreciate the great talent of the early stars in depicting emotions on a silent screen with only subtitles to assist.

And, yes...as is so often quoted from the movie *Sunset Boulevard*..."They had faces then." Such faces...distinctive and extraordinarily mobile, many of great beauty, and capable of reducing an audience in a darkened theater to tears. Many of these faces were used on sheet music covers to publicize the movies, and the following accumulation shows both famous stars and obscure ingénues as they appeared during their prime, forgotten perhaps by a once adoring public. We have not forgotten, and hope that this exhibit will perpetuate their contribution to historical cinema. For ease in location, the stars are listed alphabetically.

Opposite page:
That Night in Araby
Rudolph Valentino with his smoldering bedroom eyes and dark good looks was a legendary silent film idol, the darling of American women. He gazes from the cover of a song from his last movie *The Son of the Sheik*. (1926)

☆ ☆ ☆ ☆ ☆

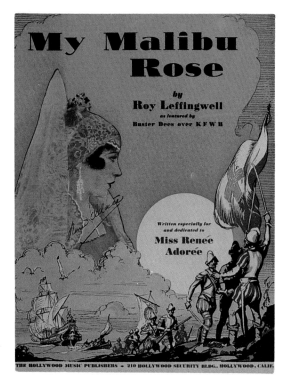

Right:
If I Ever Get a Job Again
After the trial **Arbuckle** wanted to perform but was forced into retirement by an unforgiving public, and he never again acted in movies. He did manage to find work as a director under the pseudonym William B. Goodrich, making a few shorts and two feature films. He died broken-hearted a year after this song was written. (1932) *Collection of Harold Jacobs*

My Malibu Rose
Renée Adorée (1898-1933) had a short but active career in the movies. She was a French import, a one-time chorus girl with the Folies-Bèrgere. In Hollywood in 1925 she catapulted to stardom with her sensitive portrayal opposite John Gilbert in *The Big Parade*. She continued acting until advancing tuberculosis claimed her life at the early age of 35. Other song covers with her photo are from the 1928 movies *The Mating Call* and *The Cossacks*. (1929) *Collection of Harold Jacobs*

Below:
Rose of Monterey
Mary Astor (1906-1987) co-starred with **Gilbert Roland** in the First National movie *Rose of the Golden West*, the two shown on cover in a scene from the film. Miss Astor's career survived a monumental scandal in 1936 when her torrid diary surfaced during a child custody court battle linking her to an extramarital love affair with writer George Kaufman. Handsome Gilbert Roland (1905-1994) was a popular leading man throughout the 1920s and '30s, weathering the change to sound, and growing old gracefully while he continued his career into his seventies. (1927)

Sipping Cider Thru' a Straw
Roscoe (Fatty) Arbuckle (1887-1933) was the top funny man in Mack Sennett's Keystone comedies from 1916 to 1921. He was an enormously fat man with a round baby face who became one of Hollywood's biggest stars. His acting career was ruined after the death of young starlet Virginia Rappe whom he was accused of sexually assaulting at a wild drinking party. The country was shocked by the horror of the accusations, and Arbuckle was found guilty in Hearst's "yellow press" articles before the case even went to trial. Though he was eventually acquitted by a jury who found him free from all blame, his career never recovered from the scandal. This comedy lisping song was dedicated to him before the notoriety of the rape-murder case. (1919)

Left:
Judy
Romance of the Underworld starred **Mary Astor**, shown here on the cover of the movie theme song. Though some silent stars' careers failed with the onset of sound, Miss Astor's continued to thrive, and she made over seventy sound features. In 1941 she appeared in two memorable films, *The Maltese Falcon* with Humphrey Bogart, and *The Great Lie* with Bette Davis, for which she won an Academy Award as best supporting actress. (1928)

In the Evening by the Moonlight in Dear Old Tennessee
King Baggott (1874-1948) was a handsome stage actor who entered movies in 1911. His virile good looks made him a favorite with the ladies. He starred in many silent movies including *Ivanhoe* (1913), *Absinthe* (1914), *The Cheater* (1920), and *The Butterfly Girl* (1921). He later became a competent director of such films as *Tumbleweeds* starring William S. Hart. (1914)

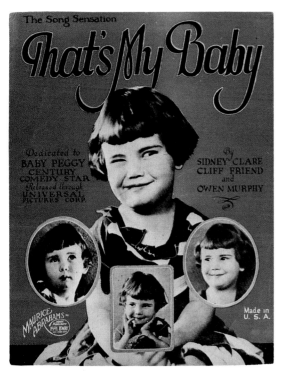

That's My Baby
Baby Peggy (Montgomery) (1918-) was a popular child star with a winning personality who appeared in 1920s movies. Between the ages of three and ten she starred in more than a dozen features, after which her popularity waned as so often happens to child stars approaching the awkward years of adolescence. In later years she wrote two books on Hollywood history under a pseudonym—*The Hollywood Posse* (1975) about movie cowboy stuntmen, and *Hollywood Children* (1979) about child stars. (1923)

Right:
The White Heather
Mabel Ballin (1887-1958) and **Ralph Graves** (1900-1977) co-starred in *The White Heather* for which this theme song was written. Lovely Miss Ballin starred in silent movies from 1917 until her retirement from the screen in 1925. Mr. Graves was a handsome athletic leading man with a long string of silents and talkies to his credit. *The White Heather* was an exciting action drama with an undersea battle and underwater scenes made possible by the use of the Williamson Submarine Tube. (1919)

THE NIGHT OF LOVE

SONG
with Ukulele Arrangement

Lyric and Music by
Vilma Banky

Jerome H. Remick & Co.
New York   Detroit
MADE IN U.S.A.

Left:
The Night of Love
Vilma Banky (1898-1991) was a talented European actress who had a successful career in Hollywood playing opposite such stellar leading men as Rudolph Valentino, Gary Cooper, and Ronald Colman. She was publicized by Samuel Goldwyn Studios as "The Hungarian Rhapsody," and in retrospect has been likened to Grace Kelly, not only for her blonde beauty, but also for her regal carriage and grace. Talented as well as beautiful, Miss Banky composed this theme song for the Goldwyn production *The Night of Love*. (1927)

☆ ☆ ☆ ☆ ☆
The Vamp, Theda Bara

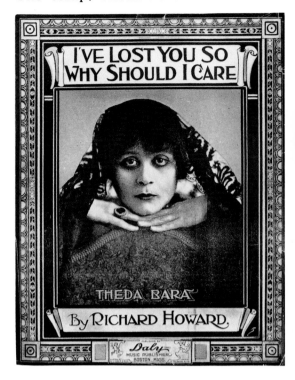

I'VE LOST YOU SO WHY SHOULD I CARE

THEDA BARA

By RICHARD HOWARD

Daly
MUSIC PUBLISHER
BOSTON, MASS.

I've Lost You So Why Should I Care
Theda Bara (1890-1955), whose real name was Theodosia Goodman, became famous as "The Vamp" after playing an enticing femme fatale in *A Fool There Was* (1915), a film based on Rudyard Kipling's novel *The Vampire*. Although she actually sprang from plebeian beginnings in Cincinnati, she was publicized in typical Hollywood studio fashion as the love child of a French artist and his Egyptian mistress. She appeared in more than 40 films, mostly playing seductive sirens, and very nearly cornered the market in vamp roles. (1916)

THIS IS HEAVEN

Theme Song for
VILMA BANKY
in
"THIS IS HEAVEN"
A
Samuel Goldwyn
Production —
Directed by
Alfred Santell

WORDS BY
JACK YELLEN
MUSIC BY
HARRY AKST

AGER, YELLEN & BORNSTEIN INC.
MUSIC PUBLISHERS
745-7TH AVE.   NEW YORK

This Is Heaven
This Is Heaven was a silent movie to which Sam Goldwyn added some sound sequences. Despite her daily English lessons, **Vilma Banky** was plagued with a thick Hungarian accent that doomed her career in movies with dialogue. The picture lost money, and she retired from the movies in 1930. In real life she was married to handsome screen actor Rod La Rocque for over forty years. Miss Banky was an invalid for ten years before her death, and was so upset when no one visited her that she asked that no notice be given of her death. Alone and forgotten, she died in 1991 in a Los Angeles nursing home at the age of about ninety, and had her ashes scattered at sea. (1929)

Right:
In Egypt
Wild-eyed and scantily-clad, **Theda Bara** is seen on this cover as Egypt's queen in a scene from *Cleopatra*, complete with a tame lion curled on the steps. Off-screen she enjoyed the role of a star, creating an unforgettable impression as she rode with exotic hauteur in a white limousine attended by Nubian footmen. She added to the mystique by holding press interviews in dimly-lit rooms hung with heavy black velvet draperies and scented with incense, and surrounding herself with unusual pets. (1918)
Collection of James Nelson Brown

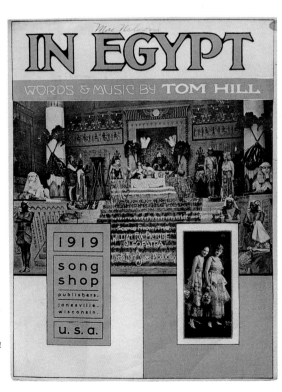

IN EGYPT
WORDS & MUSIC BY TOM HILL

1919
song
shop
publishers,
Janesville,
Wisconsin.
u. s. a.

Scene from the
WILLIAM FOX PICTURE
CLEOPATRA

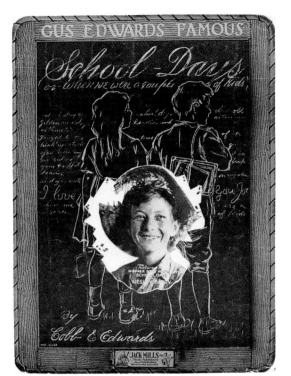

School Days

Wesley Barry (born 1907) was the freckle-faced lad who appeared in five features with Mary Pickford before coming into his own as the star of *Dinty* in 1920. In Warner Brothers' silent movie *School Days* he played a youngster who chooses a life of big city crime until he sees the error of his ways and returns to his own small home town. Barry later turned to the production side of movies. (1925)

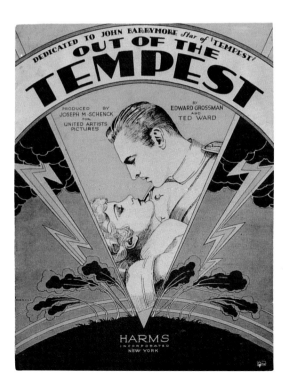

Right:
Madrigal of May from *The Jest*
John Barrymore (1882-1942), known as the "Great Profile," was an accomplished stage actor with a magnificent speaking voice, at his best in Shakespearean roles. He entered the movies in 1913, equally at ease in dramatic, comedy, or adventure parts. On the stage he starred in *The Jest*, singing this song composed by Maurice Nitke. This edition, autographed by the composer at top of page, is inscribed to actor Henry Hull. (1919)

Bottom right:
Eternal Love
Despite fine reviews praising the excellent acting of **John Barrymore** and **Camilla Horn**, *Eternal Love* was a box-office dud. The photography, shot in the Canadian Rockies, was superb, and the story was good—about lovers fleeing from murder charges into the snowy mountains, only to perish in an avalanche—but the movie suffered, mainly because it had no spoken dialogue—only sound effects, in a year of public clamor for talking pictures. (1929)
Collection of James Nelson Brown

Left:
Out of the Tempest
The movie *Tempest*, United Artists' first film with synchronized music and sound effects, was a smash hit. It was a period picture set during the 1914 Bolshevik uprising, and it starred **John Barrymore** with **Camilla Horn**. Barrymore successfully made the transition to sound movies, but years of heavy drinking took their toll; he suffered from memory lapses, and his handsome features reflected his dissipated life style. (1928)

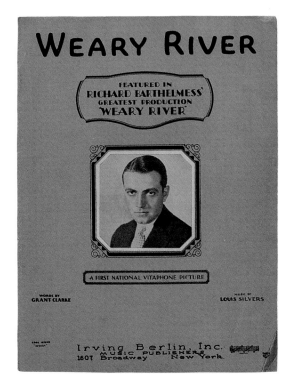

Left:

Humpty Dumpty Heart
The sound movie *Playmates*
was **John Barrymore**'s last
movie before his death in a
performance some have
described as a sad spectacle, a
caricature of himself as a
has-been actor trying to make
a comeback. With billing
below Kay Kyser, it was a big
step down from Barrymore's
early Shakespearean grandeur.
Songs were by James Van
Heusen and Johnny Burke.
(1941)

☆ ☆ ☆ ☆ ☆

Right:

Beggars of Life
In silent movies **Wallace Beery**
(1885-1949) was famous for his
"Sweedie" Series in which he
appeared in drag, continuing
with a lengthy career in both
silents and talkies. He played a
gruff but kind-hearted leader of
a hobo camp in Paramount's
first feature movie using the
spoken word. He is shown here
on the cover of the theme song
from *Beggars of Life*. Beery won a
best actor Academy Award for
his performance as a down and
out boxer in *The Champ* in
1931-32. (1928)

Weary River
Richard Barthelmess (1895-1963) was one of D. W.
Griffith's heroes in *Broken Blossoms* and *Way Down
East*. Not only handsome and virile-looking, he was an
excellent actor, nominated for the best acting
Academy Award at the first awards banquet for his
performances in *The Noose* and *The Patent Leather Kid*.
He appears on the cover of the title song of the part-
talkie *Weary River*, in which he portrayed a convict.
(1929)

The Eternal City of Dreams
Lionel Barrymore (1878-1954) was a distinguished stage actor, and the first of
the famous Barrymore family to appear in films. He acted in some of D. W.
Griffith's early movies, and in Pearl White's *Elaine* serials, but also continued
on the stage until 1926 when he signed a contract with M-G-M. He played a
few leading man roles eventually moving into meatier character parts such as
crusty Dr. Gillespie in the *Dr. Kildare* series in the 1930s. He won an Academy
Award for best actor in *A Free Soul* in 1930-31. **Barbara La Marr** (1896-1926) is
the beauty who appears with Barrymore on the cover of the theme song from
The Eternal City. Her life ended tragically at age 29 from an overdose of
narcotics. (1923) *Collection of Harold Jacobs*

114

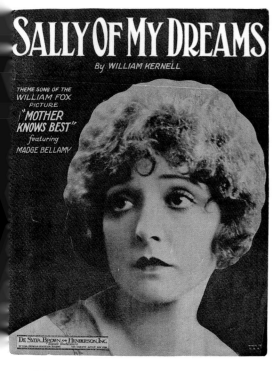

SALLY OF MY DREAMS

By WILLIAM KERNELL

THEME SONG OF THE
WILLIAM FOX
PICTURE
"MOTHER
KNOWS BEST"
featuring
MADGE BELLAMY

Left:
Sally of My Dreams
Madge Bellamy (1900-) played sweet innocent roles in silent movies and early talkies, appearing on the cover of the theme song from the William Fox picture *Mother Knows Best*. Her best known portrayals were in the silent movies *Lorna Doone* and *The Iron Horse*. (1928)

Below:
Flower of Love
In *White Shadows in the South Seas*, **Monte Blue** (1890-1963) portrayed a drunken doctor who reforms and tries to protect an idyllic primitive society from civilization's evils. He appears on the cover in a passionate embrace with co-star **Racquel Torres**. Though touted as M-G-M's first sound picture, it was actually a silent movie with added synchronized sound effects and music. Filmed on location in the Marquesas Islands in the South Pacific, its beautiful cinematography won the 1929 Academy Award. Monte Blue enjoyed a long career in movies, first as a leading man, later playing character roles into the 1950s. Miss Torres made a handful of talkies including *The Sea Bat* and *Under a Texas Moon* before retiring from films in the 1930s. (1928)

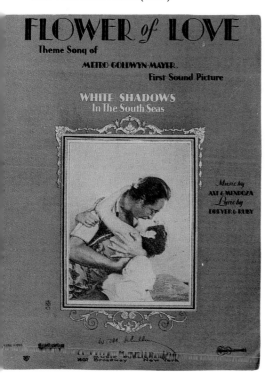

FLOWER of LOVE

Theme Song of
METRO-GOLDWYN-MAYER
First Sound Picture

WHITE SHADOWS
In The South Seas

☆ ☆ ☆ ☆ ☆
The "IT" Girl, Clara Bow

"IT"
NOVELTY FOX-TROT

DEDICATED TO
CLARA BOW
STAR OF THE PARAMOUNT PICTURE
"IT"

WORDS AND
MUSIC BY
Will Wright
AND
Al. Purrington

AVON MUSIC PUB. CO.
AVON, N.J.

"It"
Clara Bow (1906-1965) was the personification of the jazz baby of the 1920s, a saucy, wanton flapper with bobbed hair and cupid bow lips. She was sensational in Paramount's *"It"* portraying a shopgirl in love with her boss, a rich department store owner. Writer Elinor Glyn described "It" as "that peculiar quality which some persons possess, which attracts others of the opposite sex. The possessor of 'It' must be absolutely un-selfconscious, and must have that magnetic 'sex appeal' which is irresistible." Miss Bow fit the description, and rose to superstardom as the "It" girl. (1927) *Collection of Roy Bishop*

Right:
Red Hair
Clara Bow played a gold-digging manicurist in *Red Hair*, again dominating the screen with her sparkling personality and special magnetism. A much-publicized scene from the movie shows her in a fit of pique stripping to her lingerie and jumping into a swimming pool at a fancy party. In real life, Miss Bow married cowboy star Rex Bell who later became lieutenant governor of Nevada, but she was unable to participate in public functions, suffering from mental instability that kept her in and out of sanitariums for many years. (1928) *Collection of Harold Jacobs*

RED HAIR

With
UKULELE
Arrangement

By
Alfred Bryan
Francis Wheeler
& Ted Snyder

Dedicated to CLARA BOW
by
ELINOR GLYN
A PARAMOUNT PICTURE

115

Right:
I'm Sorry I Made You Cry
John Bowers (1899-1936) was a handsome leading man in silent movies who failed to make the transition to talkies, and ended up an alcoholic who committed suicide by drowning. The movie *A Star Is Born* is said to be loosely based on the Bowers story. **June Elvidge** (1893-1965) was a vaudeville, stage, and screen actress who made silent movies from 1915 to 1924. The two stars appear on the cover of a popular song from World War I. (1918)

My Wild Party Girl
Provocatively cute and exuding an earthy sex appeal, **Clara Bow** was featured by Paramount in a speaking role in *The Wild Party* portraying a wild collegian using her wiles on an attractive professor portrayed by Fredric March. (1929)

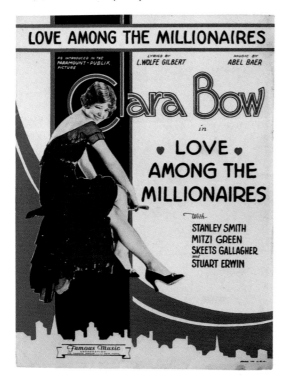

Love Among the Millionaires
Clara Bow played a cafe waitress in *Love Among the Millionaires*, an early talking picture by Paramount-Publix that also starred Stanley Smith and Stuart Erwin. Scandalous rumors of her sexual escapades were blamed for the demise of her career which ended shortly after two or three sound movies. (1930)

Consolation
William Boyd (1898-1972) was a rugged hero type in many silent movies of the 1920s before he embarked on a new phase of acting as the popular Western hero Hopalong Cassidy. This theme song from Cecil B. De Mille's production of *Dress Parade* co-starred Bessie Love and Mr. Boyd in his pre-Hopalong days. (1926)

Left:
Loveland
Alice Brady (1892-1939) was a dramatic actress who played attractive silent screen heroines. She made a smooth transition to sound movies in the 1930s playing character roles, and won an Academy Award as best supporting actress in 1938 for her performance in *In Old Chicago*. (1919)

Peter Pan
Betty Bronson (1906-1971) was chosen by Sir James Barrie to star in the first film version of his enchanting play *Peter Pan*. Cast as the boy who never grew up, she became an immediate star, but though she subsequently made many silents and early talkies, permanent stardom eluded her. Other films in which she appeared were *Ben Hur* (1926, as the Virgin Mary), *A Kiss for Cinderella* (1926), and the early talkie *Sonny Boy* (1929). She married and retired in the early 1930s, but returned in 1937 to work in a Gene Autry movie, and also appeared in some later character roles. (1924)

Right:
Good Gracious Annabelle
Billie Burke (1885-1970) starred in several silent movies including the romantic comedy *Good Gracious Annabelle*. She also had a successful career in talking pictures including the role of Glinda, the Good Fairy, in *The Wizard of Oz* (1939). Later roles into the late 1950s found her type-cast as an air-headed bubbly comedienne. (1919)

The Girl of the Olden West
Sylvia Breamer (1898-1943) was an Australian-born actress described by a contemporary as "a dark and slumbrous beauty." She was a busy actress during the 1920s with many screen credits including *The Narrow Trail* (1917), *My Lady's Garter* (1920), *Doubling for Romeo* (1922), and *Up in Mabel's Room* (1926). She is shown on the cover of the theme song from the First National picture *The Girl of the Golden West*. (1923)

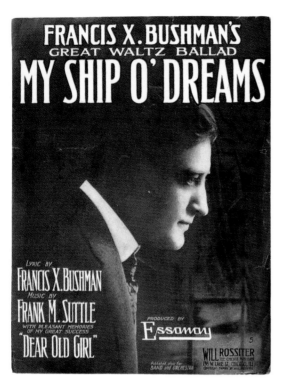

Left:

My Ship O' Dreams
Francis X. Bushman (1883-1966) was a popular romantic lead in pre-1920 movies for Essanay studio, and a great favorite with the ladies. His handsome profile is seen on the cover of this song for which he wrote the lyrics and Frank M. Suttle, the music. His most famous role was Messala in the 1926 silent version of *Ben Hur* in which he refused to use a double for the dangerous chariot race at the end of the film. (1915)

Somewhere There's Someone
June Caprice (1899-1936) was a William Fox screen star of the mid-teens who played bright-eyed innocents along the lines of Mary Pickford. Her pre-1920 silent films include *Caprice of the Mountains*, *A Modern Cinderella*, *The Love Cheat*, and *A Damsel In Distress*. She also appeared in the ten-chapter serial *Pirate Gold* in 1920, and played the female lead in *The Sky Ranger* (1921), a fifteen chapter serial by Pathé. (1918)

Right:

Sweet Sue Just You
Sue Carol (1907-1982) played a bouncy flapper in films of the late 1920s and early 1930s, after which she retired to become a talent agent. Among her discoveries was 1940s screen idol Alan Ladd who became her fourth husband. Her movies include *Slaves of Beauty* (1927), *The Cohens and Kellys in Paris* (1928), and *The Exalted Flapper* (1929). (1928)

You Didn't Want Me When You Had Me
Catherine Calvert (1891-1971) was a lovely brunette leading lady of both the stage and screen. She made about a dozen silent movies from 1917 to 1922 including *Behind the Mask*, *A Romance of the Underworld*, and *Fires of Faith*. This cover photo was taken the year she starred in *The Career of Catherine Bush*. (1919)

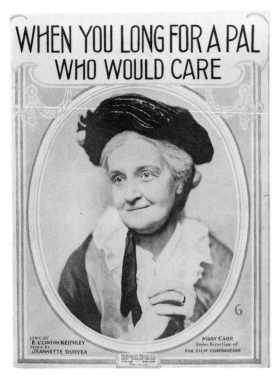

WHEN YOU LONG FOR A PAL WHO WOULD CARE

LYRIC BY
E. CLINTON KEITHLEY
MUSIC BY
JEANNETTE DURYEA

MARY CARR
Under Direction of
FOX FILM CORPORATION

McKINLEY MUSIC CO.

Left:
When You Long for a Pal Who Would Care
Mary Carr (1874-1973) was a familiar face in silent movies. She was a veteran of the stage who came to the silver screen as a grey-haired middle-aged character actress in 1918. She made a splash in *Mrs. Wiggs of the Cabbage Patch* in 1919 and attracted favorable notice the following year in *Over the Hill to the Poorhouse*. As a kindly motherly type she was unsurpassed, and starred in films well into the 1930s. (1922)

I'M ALL A-TWITTER

WORDS BY
LEO ROBIN
MUSIC BY
RICHARD A. WHITING

THEME SONG OF
THE PARAMOUNT PRODUCTION
"CLOSE HARMONY"

BUDDY ROGERS

NANCY CARROLL

FAMOUS MUSIC
CORPORATION
SOLE SELLING AGENTS
HARMS
NEW YORK

I'm All A-Twitter
Nancy Carroll poses coquettishly with dashing **Charles "Buddy" Rogers** on the cover of this theme song from Paramount's all-talking movie *Close Harmony*. Miss Carroll was a talented singer and dancer, and the addition of sound to movies was a boon to her career which sky-rocketed in the 1930s. Her acting ability was recognized with an Academy Award nomination in 1930 for her sensitive portrayal of a young manicurist who chooses love over money in *The Devil's Holiday*. (1929)

The Man of a Thousand Faces, Lon Chaney

ROSEMARY

Lyrics by
ANNE NICHOLS
Music by
J. S. ZAMECNIK.

FROM
ANNE NICHOLS
"ABIE'S IRISH ROSE"
Paramount's
Supreme Motion Picture Achievement

SAM FOX PUB. CO.

Rosemary
Nancy Carroll (1904-1965) worked on the Broadway stage before entering the movies late in the silent era. Paramount hired her and Charles "Buddy" Rogers to play the Irish bride and Jewish groom in the movie version of Anne Nichols' hit Broadway play, *Abie's Irish Rose*. They were a charismatic couple, and subsequently made three more pictures together. Miss Carroll smiles from the center of a rose on the theme song cover. (1928)

Right:
Ching, Ching, Chinaman
Silent screen actor **Lon Chaney** (1883-1930) became famous as "The Man of a Thousand Faces" for his ability to transform his facial features. He was the son of deaf-mute parents, and learned early in life to communicate with them through gesture and facial expression—skills that later proved invaluable in his screen career. He became an authority on makeup, and wrote the makeup entry for an edition of the *Encyclopedia Brittanica*. This striking song cover from *Shadows* shows his makeup expertise. (1922) *Collection of Harold Jacobs*

CHING, CHING, CHINAMAN
SONG
Lyric by EVE UNSELL   Music by LOUIS F. GOTTSCHALK

Lon Chaney
as
CHING
CHING
CHINAMAN
in
the

"SHADOWS"

SCREEN PRODUCTION

JEROME H. REMICK & CO.
NEW YORK   DETROIT

The Miracle Man

Left:
The Miracle Man
The Miracle Man was another worthy vehicle for the talents of **Lon Chaney**. A group of swindlers led by Thomas Meighan tried to cash in on religious faith, and Chaney played a fake cripple who crawls to the feet of the village miracle man, played by Joseph Dowling, and is miraculously "cured." The faith of a nearby crippled boy creates a real miracle when he throws away his crutches and walks. Chaney's extraordinary gifts extended even to his brilliant portrayal of the cripple with crooked limbs in this movie. (1919)

Charlie Chaplin Walk
Charlie Chaplin (1889-1977) was one of the greatest screen clowns of all time. He created and refined the lovable character of Charlie the Tramp, as seen here on a sheet music cover. At the first Academy Award presentation in 1927-28, Chaplin was awarded a special Oscar "for versatility and genius in writing, acting, directing, and producing *The Circus*." A further tribute to Chaplin was knighthood by the Queen of England in 1975. (1915)

Right:
Those Charlie Chaplin Feet
Charlie Chaplin mugs for the camera on the cover of this song with words by Edgar Leslie to music by Archie Gottler. Bailey and Cowan, also seen on cover, featured the song in their act. (1915)

Laugh Clown Laugh
Lon Chaney shows another of his "thousand faces" on the cover of the movie theme song for *Laugh Clown Laugh*. In this silent movie he portrayed a sad circus clown in love with a young woman who is in love with someone else. Bandleader Ted Fiorito composed the title theme with lyrics by Sam Lewis and Joe Young, and the song became very popular, topping the 1928 Hit Parade. (1928)

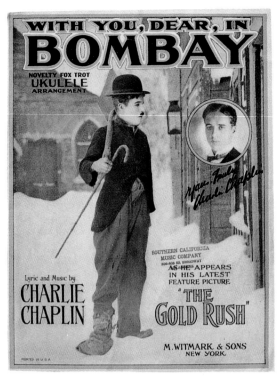

Left:

With You, Dear, in Bombay
As the little tramp, **Charlie Chaplin** appears on the cover of a song from his movie *The Gold Rush*. He was proud of this movie, and is quoted as saying, "This is the picture I want to be remembered by." As a bumbling prospector in Alaska's gold country Charlie is stranded during a snowstorm, and resorts to cooking and eating his shoe in a very funny scene. Chaplin wrote this song for the movie. (1925)

Carmen
Charlie Chaplin took the wind out of Cecil B. De Mille's sails with his burlesque of De Mille's grandiose silent drama, *Carmen* that starred opera singer Geraldine Farrar. Chaplin's two-reel version was his last film with Essanay, and he was chagrined to find after he left that they put in all the cut-outs and extended it to four reels. He stated in his autobiography, "Although this was a dishonest act, it rendered a service, for thereafter I had it stipulated in every contract that there should be no mutilating, extending or interfering with my finished work." Chaplin is seen with co-star **Edna Purviance** (1894-1958) on the cover of the movie theme song. (1916 movie) *Collection of James Nelson Brown*

Sing a Song
A young and good-looking **Charlie Chaplin** poses on the cover of another song he helped compose for his movie triumph, *The Gold Rush*. Chaplin was musically inclined, playing both violin and cello, and practiced diligently, with great ambitions to be a concert artist. Though that dream didn't materialize, he used his innate talent to write music for his movies. "I tried to compose elegant and romantic music to frame my comedies in contrast to the tramp character, for elegant music gave my comedies an emotional dimension." Other songs he composed include "Eternally" for *Limelight*, and "Smile" for *Modern Times*. (1925) *Collection of James Nelson Brown*

✩ ✩ ✩ ✩ ✩

Right:

Marguerite Clark Waltz
Marguerite Clark (1887-1940) was a major star at Famous Players, making 39 silent movies until her retirement in 1921. Her first major success as the heroine in *Wildflower* (1914) was followed by other starring roles including the dual title role in *The Prince and the Pauper* (1915) and the dual role of Topsy and Eva in *Uncle Tom's Cabin* (1918). Sadly, none of her films are available today for viewing. (1917)

Left:

I Want a Dixie Sweetheart
Marguerite Clark, a petite beauty with brown hair and hazel eyes, was a legitimate actress coming to films from the stage. With her air of sweetness and innocence, she rivalled Mary Pickford in popularity. She is fondly remembered and highly praised for two fairy tale films made for Christmas audiences— *Snow White* (1916) and *The Seven Swans* (1917). She is seen here on the cover of a Knapp Company lithograph. (1919)

That Beloved Cheater of Mine
Lew Cody (1884-1934) was a handsome debonair actor who was married to Mabel Normand at the time of her early death. He knew her from the days they co-starred in *Mickey*, when Cody played the role of the villain in the piece. Cody died four years after Normand from a heart ailment. He is seen on the cover of this theme song from the movie *The Beloved Cheater*. (1920)

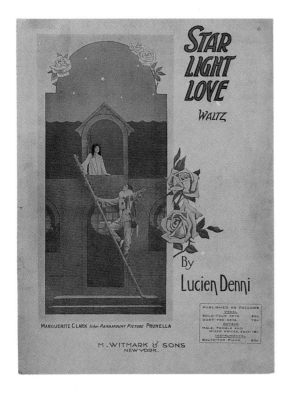

Right:

A Thief in Paradise
After service on the French front in World War I, **Ronald Colman** (1891-1958) turned to acting, eventually drifting into movies in England. He came to the United States in 1920 and was discovered by Lillian Gish who wanted him for her leading man in *The White Sister*. He was an immediate success, and became one of Hollywood's most popular romantic stars. (1925)

Star Light Love
Prunella was said to be **Marguerite Clark**'s finest movie, and French director Maurice Tourneur was also praised for his sensitive direction. The story, based on a play by Laurence Houseman and Granville Barker, was a romance about a Paris actress. Miss Clark originally played the part on the stage, and so impressed Adolph Zukor that he offered her fifty times what she was presently earning to star in movies. Cover scene shows her being wooed by actor Jules Raucort. (1919) *Collection of Harold Jacobs*

Left:
Beau Geste
Beau Geste was the exciting tale of three brothers in the Foreign Legion with **Ronald Colman** in the lead and Neil Hamilton and Ralph Forbes as the other brothers. The climax of the movie showed 40 Legionnaires trying to fend off a fierce attack by 4,000 Arabs. Musical themes from the movie were composed by Hugo Riesenfeld. (1927)

To Have and to Hold
Betty Compson (1897-1974) and **Bert Lytell** (1885-1954) co-starred in Paramount's *To Have and to Hold*, a historical romance set in the American colonies. Miss Compson was a beautiful blonde who started out in Al Christie's film comedies before hitting the big time with a dramatic starring role opposite Lon Chaney in *The Miracle Man*. She made over 150 films in a long career that included both silents and talkies. Mr. Lytell was a popular actor on stage, screen, radio, and television, and portrayed the Lone Wolf in several movies. (1922)

☆ ☆ ☆ ☆ ☆

"The Kid," Jackie Coogan

Right:
Peck's Bad Boy
Jackie Coogan (1914-1984) became an immediate star when he was featured by Charlie Chaplin in *The Kid* in 1921. The earnest bright-eyed raggedy little boy beguiled audiences, who placed him in the forefront of celebrities until he entered his teens. He is seen here as the waif he portrayed in the silent movie *Peck's Bad Boy*. (1921)

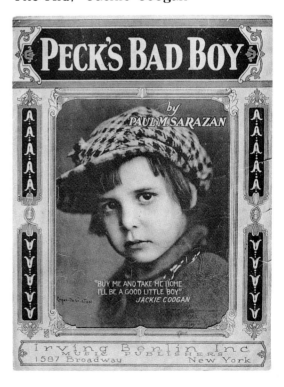

The Magic Flame
Ronald Colman was a frequent co-star of **Vilma Banky** in silent films. They appear on the cover of the title song from their fourth movie together, *The Magic Flame*. Colman played a dual role—a circus clown and a Crown Prince, and Miss Banky played an aerial acrobat. (1927)

Left:
Oliver Twist
Charles Dickens' masterpiece *Oliver Twist* was a perfect vehicle for winsome **Jackie Coogan** who portrayed the lead with great sincerity and pathos. He is seen here on the theme song cover begging for "...some more." Both lyrics and music were composed by Vaughn De Leath. (1922)

☆ ☆ ☆ ☆ ☆

The First Kiss
Gary Cooper (1901-1961) started out in silents as a cowboy extra in Westerns, but made his mark as second lead in Samuel Goldwyn's *The Winning of Barbara Worth* in 1926. He became an enduring superstar, winning Academy Awards for the movies *Sergeant York* and *High Noon*. He is seen here with **Fay Wray** on the cover of the silent movie, *The First Kiss*, in which he portrayed a poor fisherman who gets into trouble with the law. (1928)

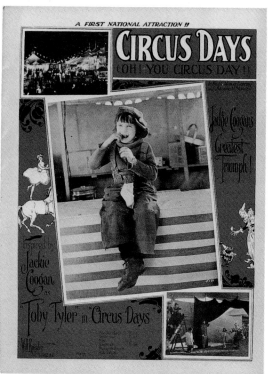

Right:
A Precious Little Thing Called Love
A Shopworn Angel was made as a silent movie, but was withdrawn to have some incongruous dialogue and sound effects added to keep up with the demand for spoken word in films. **Gary Cooper** played a soldier in love with a Broadway show girl, played by **Nancy Carroll**. Cooper had seven lines of dialogue near the end of the picture, and Nancy Carroll sang this theme song. (1928)

Circus Days
Jackie Coogan starred as Toby Tyler in the First National silent movie *Circus Days*. He appears in character in scenes from the movie on this theme song cover. Coogan was a gifted little actor, and will always be remembered as the appealing "kid" he played in silent movies. (1923)

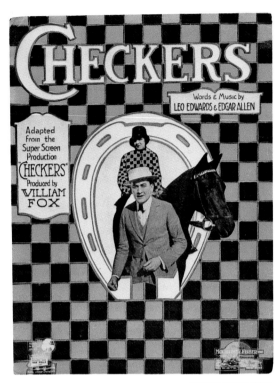

Right:
Checkers
Thomas Corrigan was a star for Selig Polyscope Company as early as 1912. He appears with the young horsewoman **Jean Acker** on this song cover from the William Fox movie *Checkers*. Miss Acker was Rudolph Valentino's first wife, and even after their separation and divorce she continued to use his name to promote herself (unsuccessfully) in movies. (1919)

Evangeline
Miriam Cooper (1891-1976) played memorable roles in D. W. Griffith's *The Birth of a Nation* and *Intolerance*, and starred in many films from 1916 to 1926. This theme song was written for the Fox movie *Evangeline*, based on Longfellow's poem. Late in life Miss Cooper published her autobiography, *Dark Lady of the Silents*, an insightful look at life in early Hollywood. (1919)

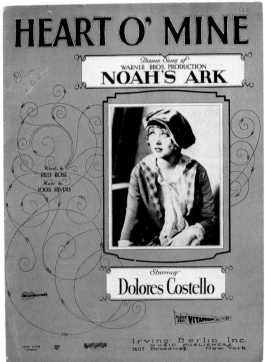

Left;
Girl of My Dreams
Miriam Cooper, unidentified on this cover, was considered one of Hollywood's great beauties during her heyday. She was also an accomplished actress, and was most proud of her work in the 1917 movie *The Honor System*, a shockingly realistic movie about the dehumanization of convicts in a sordid prison atmosphere. It was instrumental in starting a humanitarian movement in prison reform based on the honor system that Governor W. P. Hunt instituted in Arizona. Unfortunately the film was destroyed in the 1937 fire at Fox studios. (1919)

Heart O' Mine
Beautiful **Dolores Costello** (1905-1979) was Maurice Costello's daughter, and worked with him and her sister Helene in several early Vitagraph films. After her schooling, she did some modeling and dancing on the stage before returning to films. She co-starred in *The Sea Beast* (1926) with her future husband John Barrymore, and made many fine films well into the sound era. *Noah's Ark* was a part-talkie film with the first part silent. The movie was fraught with misfortune when the disastrous Biblical floodwaters went awry and several extras were drowned. (1928)

Left:
I Loved You Then
Joan Crawford (1904-1977) started life as Lucille Le Sueur, and became a professional dancer after she won a Charleston contest. She was discovered by M-G-M while dancing in a Broadway chorus line, and was groomed for stardom. With her new name of Joan Crawford, she made a number of silent movies including *Our Dancing Daughters*, in which she was cast as a gay seductive flapper. (1928)

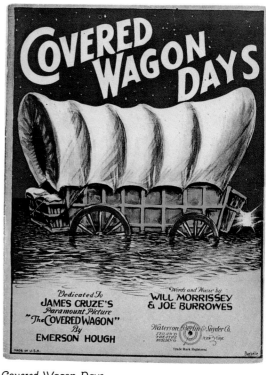

Covered Wagon Days
James Cruze (1884-1942), director of *The Covered Wagon*, took his company to Snake Valley, Nevada, where they established a camp of five hundred tents. He recruited extras from the "locals," and spent eight weeks shooting spectacular location sequences. The movie was a huge success, the first big epic Western, and it started a cycle of pictures depicting American pioneer life that brought both history and drama to the silent screen. (1923)

Right:
Westward Ho!
This march song was inspired by and dedicated to the Jesse L. Lasky film *The Covered Wagon*. Hugo Riesenfeld composed the music, and R. A. Barnet wrote the rallying lyrics. **James Cruze** was praised for his direction of the film, as was Karl Brown for his wonderful photography of vast stretches of the wagon train winding across the plains, fording rivers, and driving forward through heavy snows and hostile Indian attacks. (1923)

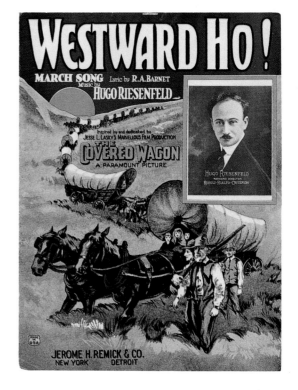

I've Waited a Lifetime for You
Our Modern Maidens starred **Joan Crawford** in what was to be her last silent film. The popular star was wed to Douglas Fairbanks Jr. in the movie as well as in real life. Moving into more mature roles in the 1940s, Miss Crawford reached superstardom with a best actress Oscar for her moving performance in *Mildred Pierce* in 1945. She was an enduring star, and made movies well into her sixties. (1929)

Left:

There's No End to My Love for You
Dorothy Dalton (1894-1972) starred in Paramount's romantic drama *Love Letters*, and is seen embracing actor **William Conklin** on the cover of this ballad. Miss Dalton was discovered by Thomas Ince while acting on the stage with a touring company in Los Angeles, and made many movies in the late 'teens and 1920s under his tutelage. Mr. Conklin (1877-1935) was an active leading man in other silent movies including *Love Madness*, *Brute Master*, and *The Other Woman*. (1917) *Collection of James Nelson Brown*

Glimpses of the Moon
Bebe Daniels (1886-1934) started her career with the Selig company as a child actress, later moving into adult roles. She was Harold Lloyd's leading lady before becoming a popular Paramount contract star in 1919. She smiles enticingly from the cover of the theme song for *Glimpses of the Moon*. The movie, based on a popular Edith Wharton novel, was advertised on the back cover, "A deluxe production of a world's best-seller. Marvelous gowns, gorgeous locations, enthralling love scenes!" Miss Daniels was a passable singer, and she and husband Ben Lyon had a successful radio show in England during the 1930s. (1923)

Right:
Salvation Rose
Millionaire publisher William Randolph Hearst fell in love with **Marion Davies** (1897-1961) when she was a young chorus girl in the *Ziegfeld Follies*. He groomed her for movie stardom, and formed his own movie company, Cosmopolitan Pictures, to produce her films. Though gifted in comedy roles, Miss Davies was frequently miscast as an innocent, virginal heroine, such as the Salvation Army Lassie in *The Belle of New York*. (1919)

The Willow Tree
Viola Dana (1898-1987) was only thirteen years old when she made her screen debut with her sister, Shirley Mason, in an Edison film *A Christmas Carol*. She became a leading star with Metro during the silent era, and starred in more than a dozen features from 1916-1924. She appears on the cover of the theme song from the Metro movie *The Willow Tree*. Miss Dana's career, like so many others, foundered with the advent of sound. (1920)

Left:
The Marion Davies March
Victor Herbert composed this march especially for the Cosmopolitan production *When Knighthood Was in Flower*, another of **Marion Davies'** extravagantly mounted silent movies. During her movie career, she appeared in over forty films, but was more famous as Hearst's paramour and hostess at the fabulous Hearst Castle in San Simeon, California, where grand parties were held and invitations were coveted. (1922)
Collection of Harold Jacobs

Tell Me Why
Priscilla Dean (1896-1988) came from a theatrical family, and cut her teeth while on tour with her parents. Already a professional actress at age fourteen, she made her screen debut at Biograph, gradually getting stronger roles including the part of the heroine, Morn Light, opposite the master criminal Harry Carter in *The Gray Ghost*, a 16 episode serial released by Universal in 1917. (1919)

Right:
I'm Goin' to Break that Mason-Dixon Line
Silent film stars **Priscilla Dean** and **Thurston Hall** (1883-1958) posed in an intense embrace for this promotional cover sponsored by Universal Film Mfg. Co. Miss Dean was an accomplished actress in silent dramas, and Mr. Hall acted on both stage and screen, appearing in hundreds of Hollywood films through the years as a character actor. (1919)

Lights of Old Broadway
The costume drama *Lights of Old Broadway* made a tidy profit for Cosmopolitan Pictures. The movie's theme song was dedicated to its star, pretty, wide-eyed **Marion Davies** who appears on the attractive cover. She played the dual role of orphan twins in the movie, showing her versatility as well as her beauty. (1925)
Collection of Roy Bishop

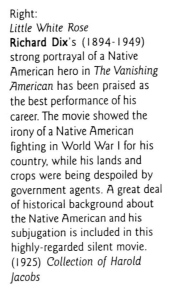

Right:
Little White Rose
Richard Dix's (1894-1949) strong portrayal of a Native American hero in *The Vanishing American* has been praised as the best performance of his career. The movie showed the irony of a Native American fighting in World War I for his country, while his lands and crops were being despoiled by government agents. A great deal of historical background about the Native American and his subjugation is included in this highly-regarded silent movie. (1925) *Collection of Harold Jacobs*

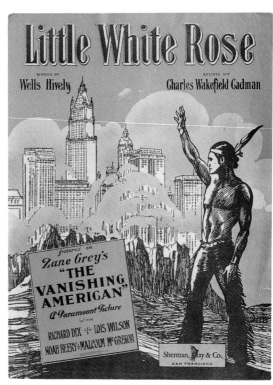

Estrellita
Dolores Del Rio (1905-1983) was a convent-educated Mexican beauty with classic features and exquisite big brown eyes. She starred in many silent films usually typecast as an exotic foreigner. This theme song from the silent movie *The Loves of Carmen* shows her on cover with co-star **Victor McLaglen**. (1927)

Evangeline
Dolores Del Rio portrayed the title role in the United Artists production *Evangeline*. This was basically a silent movie with no spoken dialogue, but had two songs sung by Miss Del Rio. Her stunning beauty enabled her to continue in sound pictures despite her Latin accent. (1929)

Out of the Dawn
Richard Dix was the prototype of the clean-cut all-American hero, and was dubbed "The Jaw" because of his strong facial bone structure. He was a popular star of the 1920s in such silent films as *The Glorious Fool* (1922) and *The Ten Commandments* (1923). He appears on the cover of the theme song from *Warming Up* in which he played a star baseball player. (1928)

Left:
Redskin
The brilliantly colored cover of this movie theme song shows **Richard Dix** done up as a Native American for *Redskin*, a movie about a Navajo who is caught between the prejudices of the white man and the American Indian. This was one of Paramount's last basically silent movies, but it had some sound and music effects added. Mr. Dix was later honored with an Academy Award nomination for best actor in the prestigious movie production *Cimarron*, but lost out to Lionel Barrymore. (1929)

Bring Back My Daddy to Me
Madge Evans (1909-1981) started out in movies at age five, and became a popular child star in silent movies. She successfully bridged the gap from adolescence to adult roles and starred in many movies through the 1930s. She appears on the cover of this plaintive World War I song through the courtesy of World Pictures. (1917)

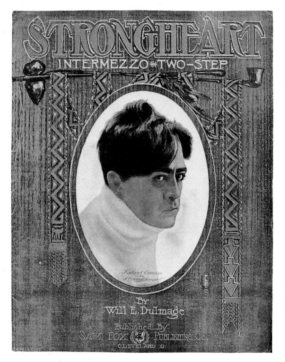

Right:
His Majesty, the American
Douglas Fairbanks (1883-1939) was an established Broadway actor when he was lured to Hollywood in 1915 to make movies. With his charm, good looks, and cheerful personality he became an immediate silent screen hero. Along with Charlie Chaplin, D. W. Griffith, and Mary Pickford, Mr. Fairbanks founded the United Artists film company in 1919. *His Majesty, the American* was the company's first film starring dashing Fairbanks as a New Yorker who fell heir to a small kingdom in Europe. The film was a great success and got the studio off to a good start. (1919)

Strongheart
Robert Edeson (1868-1931) was a stage actor who made his screen debut in 1914. He typically portrayed a stalwart hero in silent action films, later becoming a seasoned character actor. He starred in the William De Mille stage production *Strongheart* which was adapted to the screen in 1925 with its name changed to *Braveheart*. (The name was changed to avoid confusion with the first great movie star dog named Strongheart.) (1906)

OPERATIC

JUST AN OLD LOVE SONG

Theme Song
in the
Photo-Play
"DOUGLAS FAIRBANKS IN ROBIN HOOD"

WORDS BY
SID GRAUMAN
MUSIC BY
VICTOR SCHERTZINGER

Right:
A Night of Kisses
William Farnum (1876-1953) was an important star at Fox studios, and excelled in costume drama. He starred in scores of films including *The Spoilers* with his famous fight to the finish with Thomas Santschi (1914), *The Sign of the Cross* (1914), *A Tale of Two Cities* (1917), and *Les Miserables* (as Jean Valjean, 1918). At his peak he was earning $520,000 a year, and owned a seven-acre estate in the Hollywood Hills, a half-million dollar home in Maine, and two townhouses in New York City. (1919)

A NIGHT OF KISSES

BY MAX PRIVAL

WILLIAM FARNUM

KENDIS BROCKMAN MUSIC CO.

Just an Old Love Song
Swashbuckling movie idol **Douglas Fairbanks** starred in the title role in the United Artists spectacular *Robin Hood*. Fairbanks was renowned for his athletic prowess, and performed his own stunts including a leap across a 15-foot moat. Fairbanks married Mary Pickford in 1920, and the two became Hollywood's reigning king and queen, living a fairy-tale life at their lavish Hollywood estate Pickfair until their divorce in 1936. (1922)

Inspired by the William Fox Production "Wings of the Morning" starring William Farnum
POPULAR EDITION

WINGS OF THE MORNING

Words by
Jean Lefavre
Music by
W. C. Polla

C. C. CHURCH AND COMPANY, HARTFORD, CONN., U. S. A.

One For All-All For One
SONG OF THE MUSKETEERS

Lyric by
JO TRENT
Music by
HUGO RIESENFELD
and
LOUIS ALTER

DOUGLAS FAIRBANKS'
THE IRON MASK

ROBBINS MUSIC CORPORATION
799 Seventh Avenue, New York

Left:
One for All - All for One
Douglas Fairbanks was at his best starring as a devil-may-care hero in adventure epics. He exuded charm, and was good-looking and athletic. *The Iron Mask* was Fairbanks' farewell to the silent medium, and for the first time in his career, he allowed his hero to die—stabbed in the back. He wasn't pleased with the addition of sound, saying, "The romance of motion picture making ends here." (1929)

Wings of the Morning
William Farnum starred in the William Fox production of the adventurous sea yarn *Wings of the Morning*, promoted here on the sheet music theme song with a striking lithograph cover by the Knapp Company of New York. After a serious injury during the filming of *A Man Who Fights Alone* in 1924, his career faltered. His glory days were over, and he was limited to minor parts. He lost most of his fortune in the Crash of 1929, and though he continued to work in films, he ended his days in poverty. (1919)

Left:
Shadows
The beautiful and talented **Geraldine Farrar** (1882-1967) was lured to Hollywood by Lasky Features who enticed her with a private train to and from Hollywood, a house, cars, and servants plus $20,000 for eight weeks, during which three pictures were to be made. After her successful debut in the first movie *Carmen* in 1915, she stayed much longer than eight weeks. This theme song is from the Goldwyn production of *Shadows*. (1919)

Old Ironsides March
The fabulous three-masted frigate *USS Constitution* was nick-named "Old Ironsides" by the British during the War of 1812 because their shot seemed to rebound harmlessly off the hull. She is depicted on the cover of this march written by Hugo Riesenfeld for the Paramount epic movie *Old Ironsides* directed by James Cruze. **Charles Farrell** was the romantic lead. (1927)

Right:
The Gold Digger (Dig a Little Deeper)
Louise Fazenda (1895-1962) was a popular comedienne in silent movies. She got her start in Mack Sennett Keystone comedies, becoming one of his main comic stars. She starred in *The Gold Diggers*, a movie based on a Broadway stage success about Broadway show girls who are after men with money. Seen on the cover of this theme song are, left to right, Miss Fazenda, **Wyndham Standing**, and **Hope Hampton**. (1923)

Your Love Is All
Charles Farrell (b. 1901) and **Esther Ralston** (1902-1994) co-starred in Paramount's nautical action movie *Old Ironsides*. After Farrell's retirement from movies in the 1940s, he made a fortune with his exclusive Palm Springs Racquet Club, and became active in civic affairs as mayor of Palm Springs for seven years. He also starred on television's *My Little Margie* and the *Charlie Farrell Show* in the 1950s. Miss Ralston was a beautiful blonde who started out as an extra in the movies, becoming a star in the 1920s at Paramount. She appeared in dozens of films until her retirement in 1941, after which she worked in radio soap operas for a while. (1927)

Left:
Eyes of the Soul
Elsie Ferguson (1883-1961) was known as "The Aristocrat of the Screen." She brought her stage experience to the cinema, and made twenty-two movies for Paramount from 1917-1922. Unfortunately none of her films have survived. This theme song cover shows her as she appeared in the Artcraft Picture *Eyes of the Soul*. (1919)

That Melody of Love
Greta Garbo (1905-1990) emigrated to Hollywood after starting her career in the Swedish cinema, making her American screen debut in *The Torrent* in 1926. She was gifted with a commanding screen presence, both mysterious and sensual, that made her a popular film idol. Miss Garbo and co-star **John Gilbert** were linked romantically during the filming of *Love*, a movie based on Leo Tolstoy's *Anna Karenina*. It was a box-office smash. (1927)

Little Cavalier
Pauline Frederick (1881-1938) started out in show business as a chorus girl, eventually becoming a serious actress on the Broadway stage. She was summoned to Hollywood in 1915, and starred in many silent films playing a variety of leading lady roles. She brought a mature and stately charm to the screen typically in domineering mother roles, and received accolades for her acting in *Madam X* (1920) and *Smouldering Fires* (1924). She made a few sound movies in the 1930s including the successful Warner Brothers drama *Evidence* co-starring with child actor Freddie Burke Frederick. (1929)

Right:
Love's First Kiss
 Greta Garbo and **John Gilbert** are again locked in an ardent embrace on the cover of this theme song for the M-G-M silent movie *A Woman of Affairs* based on the sexy Michael Arlen novel *The Green Hat*. (1929)

133

Left:
Diane
Janet Gaynor (1906-1984) and **Charles Farrell** appear on the cover of the famous love waltz from *Seventh Heaven*, a silent movie with a synchronized musical score. Miss Gaynor won the first Academy Award ever given for best actress for her cumulative performances in three movies, *Seventh Heaven*, *Sunrise*, and *Street Angel*. The two stars were a favorite romantic couple in many movies of the 1920s and '30s. Both Mr. Farrell and Janet Gaynor did some successful television work in the fifties. (1927)

Douce Fiévre
The Big Parade was an epic wartime drama set during World War I starring **John Gilbert** and Renee Adoree, and brilliantly directed by King Vidor. The tender love story contrasts with vivid battle scenes that were lauded for their authenticity. (1927) ∨

The Gish Sisters, Dorothy and Lillian

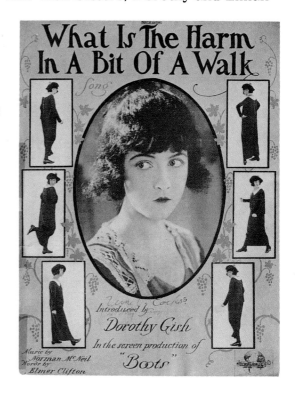

Right:
What Is the Harm in a Bit of a Walk
Dorothy Gish (1898-1968) co-starred with Richard Barthelmess in Paramount's *Boots*, a romantic comedy set in wartime London. Though her sister, Lillian, usually had the meatier roles, Dorothy was often praised as an accomplished comedienne and a fine dramatic actress. She gazes pertly from the cover of the movie theme song. (1919)
Collection of James Nelson Brown

Live and Love
John Gilbert (1897-1936) was one of the giants of the silent era. His fans adored him, and he rode a wave of popularity until the introduction of sound movies. He made ten talking pictures, but his somewhat high-pitched voice failed to suit his appearance as a virile romantic leading man, and his career lagged. He took to heavy drinking and died of a heart attack at age forty-one. He is seen on the cover of the M-G-M movie *The Masks of the Devil* with co-star **Alma Rubens**. (1928)

Left:

The Country Flapper
The Paramount-Artcraft movie *The Country Flapper* was a perfect vehicle for **Dorothy Gish**'s comedic talents. She played a flirtatious country girl who teases too many boys in a bucolic yarn based on a story *Cynic Effect* by Nalbro Bartley. This theme song is one of her loveliest covers. (1922) *Collection of Harold Jacobs*

White Blossom
D. W. Griffith composed the music for this love theme for the movie *Broken Blossoms* starring **Lillian Gish** (1898-1993). Artist Raeburn Van Buren designed the evocative cover art surrounding plaintive, fragile Miss Gish as she appeared in the movie as the pitiful child of a brutal father who beats and terrorizes her. (1919)

Right:

Love Will Forgive
Filmed on location in Sorrento, Italy, *The White Sister* stepped on the toes of Catholicism with its religious theme, but was nonetheless successful. **Lillian Gish**, believing her lover, **Ronald Colman**, has been killed in the war, enters a convent and takes her final vows as a nun. The lover returns and kidnaps her, and they go to another country and are married, but the breaking of the religious vows does not go unpunished. Miss Gish is her saintly best as the love-torn heroine, and Ronald Colman debuts handsomely in his first major role. (1923) *Collection of Harold Jacobs*

Nell Gwyn
This charming photo of **Dorothy Gish** appears on the cover of a British edition of the theme song from the silent production of *Nell Gwyn* that was filmed in England. She was well-cast as the boisterous Nell, mistress of King Charles II, and received critical praise for her interpretation. Other notable silent films in her credits include *Hearts of the World*, *Orphans of the Storm*, and *The Bright Shawl*. (1926)

135

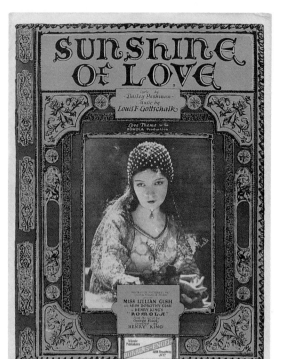

Left:
Sunshine of Love
The incredible **Lillian Gish** was an actress on both stage and screen. This song is from the Henry King epic production of *Romola* based on a novel by George Eliot about a long-suffering heroine who stoically bears the burden of a faithless husband who fathers another woman's child, another starring vehicle for Miss Gish. The setting in fifteenth century Florence was praised by Florentians for its authenticity. (1924)

Sahara
Louise Glaum (1894-1970) worked at both Pathé and Nestor studios, and attracted attention for her screen presence while working with Thomas Ince. She played effective vamp roles, notably in *Hell's Hinges* (1916) with William S. Hart. She peers seductively from the cover of the theme song from *Sahara*. (1919)

Love Brought the Sunshine
The Wind, directed by Victor Seastrom, is the story of a girl from Virginia trapped in a Texas prairie windstorm who shoots the dastardly villain, played by Montague Love, when he attacks her. **Lillian Gish** tells of the hardships she endured during the filming, "Our exteriors were shot in the desert around Bakersfield, California. Eight aeroplane propellers created the storm with the help of smoke pots and sand—temperature 120 degrees." (1928)
Collection of Harold Jacobs

Humoresque
Vera Gordon (1886-1948) and young **Bobby Connelly** promote the theme song for *Humoresque*. She typically played character parts, as she did in this movie. She was praised for her stirring performance as a poor ghetto mother who sacrificed everything to promote her young son as a successful musician. (1920)

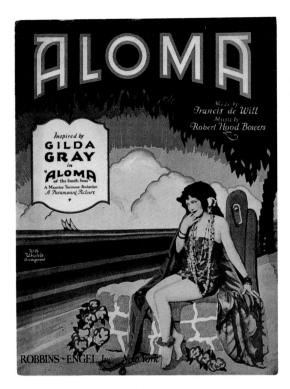

Left:
Aloma
Gilda Gray (1901-1959) was a *Ziegfeld Follies* beauty who made a few Hollywood silent movies. She achieved some fame as a shimmy dancer, and as the native girl, Aloma, she shook her grass skirt effectively in the Paramount silent movie *Aloma of the South Seas*. In 1949 Miss Gray sued Columbia studios for one million dollars, claiming that their movie *Gilda* was based on her life, and settled out of court for an undisclosed amount. (1925)

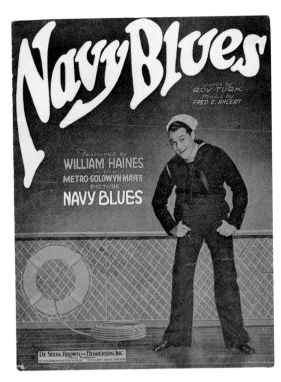

Navy Blues
William Haines (1900-1973) played light comedy roles in many 1920s movies, and moved smoothly into the sound era with this M-G-M talkie *Navy Blues*, in which he played a sailor on leave who becomes enamored of a dance-hall girl. Haines retired from the screen in the mid-1930s when his homosexuality became an embarrassment to the studio. He later became a successful interior decorator. (1929)

When Romance Wakes
The First National production *Black Oxen* co-starred **Corinne Griffith** (1894-1979) with Conway Tearle in a silent photoplay based on the best-selling novel by Gertrude Atherton. Miss Griffith moved to First National studio in Hollywood in the early 1920s, and worked for them until she retired from the screen in her thirties. She became quite a good writer after her retirement; one of her books, *Papa's Delicate Condition*, was made into a movie in 1963. (1923)

The Country Cousin
Elaine Hammerstein (1898-1948), the daughter of theatrical producer Arthur Hammerstein, started out on the stage but preferred the movies. She starred in many melodramatic silent movies from 1915 to 1926 including *The Moonstone* (1915), *The Argyle Case* (1917), *Her Man* (1918), *Souls for Sale* (1923), and *Paint and Powder* (1925), retiring in 1926 to marry an insurance executive. Songwriters Bryan and Youmans dedicated the theme song to Miss Hammerstein. (1919) *Collection of Harold Jacobs*

Left:

Left:
I'll Be Smiling When You're Crying
Despite the power and resources of her husband, Eastman Kodak executive Jules Brulatour, **Hope Hampton** (1897-1982) failed to reach stardom. She starred in a few unsuccessful silent movies including *A Modern Salome* (1920), *The Gold Diggers* (1923), and *The Truth About Women* (1924), after which she tried the world of opera where she made even less of a splash. She was never taken seriously as an actress, and became known in Hollywood, regrettably, as "Hopeless Hampton." (1921)

Darling Nellie Gray
Rugged Western hero **William S. Hart** breathed new life into the cliché ridden early Hollywood western with silent movies that are recognized even today as being the first and the best of adult Westerns. He did his own fighting in his movies, and his own expert riding on his little pinto pony, Fritz. Hart appears on cover with co-star **Eva Novak** in scenes from Paramount's *The Testing Block*. (1920)
Collection of Harold Jacobs

Right:
Salome vs. Shenandoah
Phyllis Haver (1899-1960) began her movie career in 1917 as a Mack Sennett Bathing Beauty, and in a short time was elevated to leading lady in his films. She appears seductively as the temptress Salome on the cover of the theme song from a Sennett comedy, *Salome vs. Shenandoah*. Other popular Sennett stars surround Miss Haver. (1919)
Collection of Harold Jacobs

I Want a Cave Man
William S. Hart (1870-1946) was a strong, silent type who projected an air of solid honesty in the Western silent movies for which he was famous. He started out on Broadway as a Shakespearean actor, and was middle-aged when he entered movies. He brought with him a great affection for the West and for real cowboys and Indians. He often wrote his own scripts and directed his own pictures insisting on historical accuracy in both sets and costumes. His movies were popular with audiences, and set a standard for the Western movie genre that emphasized plot over action. (1919)

Left:

Rose in the Bud

Phyllis Haver played a gold-digger after co-star Jean Hersholt's money and name in this D. W. Griffith remake of his earlier 1914 hit *Battle of the Sexes*. Griffith used a synchronized music track and sound effects in the movie, but it still came across as dated and dull. Miss Haver retired from the screen in 1929 after marrying a millionaire, but happiness eluded her, and she ended up a suicide at age 61. (1928)

The Woman Thou Gavest Me

Jack Holt (1888-1951) was an esteemed actor who was equally effective in silent movies and talkies. He started his screen career in 1913 and played leading roles well into his fifties, then continued his career as a supporting character actor. During World War II service he rose to the rank of major. He is seen here with co-star **Katherine MacDonald** on the cover of the title theme song from the movie *The Woman Thou Gavest Me*. (1919)

Right:

Pals, Just Pals

Jack Holt and **Ralph Graves** (1900-1977) co-starred in Columbia studio's first sound film which was actually a silent movie with added sound effects and a music score. They are seen on the cover of the theme song from *Submarine*. Frank Capra directed this strong, realistic movie with striking underwater photography and thrilling sequences involving an S-44 submarine and a destroyer. Holt and Graves were pals in the film, both in love with the same woman played by Dorothy Revier. (1928)

Stop Flirting

Wanda Hawley (1897-1949) was a lovely blonde leading lady in Hollywood silent movies. She frequently played seductive roles, and was purportedly one of Cecil B. De Mille's mistresses. She made dozens of silent movies from 1917 to 1927, but her career folded after the arrival of sound. Her silent films include *The Heart of a Lion* (1917), *Peg o' My Heart* (1919), and *Smouldering Fires* (1925). (1925)

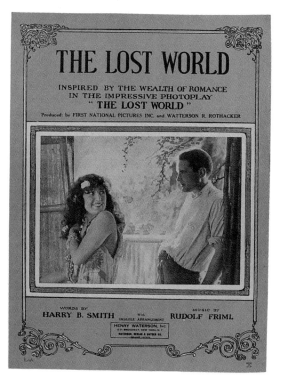

Left:
The Lost World
Lloyd Hughes (1897-1958) was a clean-cut, handsome leading man in silent films, often playing opposite Colleen Moore. He is seen with **Bessie Love** on the theme song cover for *The Lost World*, which also starred Lewis Stone and Wallace Beery. The movie was a great sci-fi flick based on Sir Arthur Conan Doyle's book about a group of explorers discovering a lost world of prehistoric monsters, with one eventually running amok in downtown London. (1925) *Collection of Harold Jacobs*

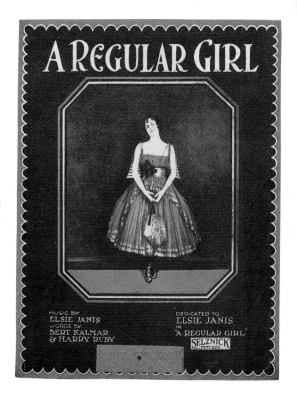

A Regular Girl
Elsie Janis (1889-1956) starred in many stage productions including *Elsie Janis and Her Gang*, in which she danced, sang, and did imitations. During the first World War she earned the title of "The Sweetheart of the AEF" for her morale-building entertainment tours in France. She also made a few silent movies including *A Regular Girl*, a Selznick Pictures' production. She is seen here on the cover of the movie's theme song that she composed with words by Bert Kalmar and Harry Ruby. (1919)

That's My Girl
Leila Hyams (1905-1977) was a popular leading lady in movies of the 1920s and '30s. She started out in her parent's vaudeville act, and her striking beauty drew her into a successful modeling career. She entered movies in 1924, and smoothly bridged the gap into talkies until her retirement in 1936. Silent films include *Sandra* (1924), *Summer Bachelors* (1926), and *The Crimson City* (1928). (1926)

Moonlight on the Danube
Leatrice Joy (1896-1985) and **Nils Asther** starred in the De Mille picture *The Blue Danube*. She was a stunning model who started as an extra in 1915, progressing to leading lady roles, usually playing career types or sophisticated society girls. She sported a boyish bobbed haircut, and she cut a dashing figure in either tailored men's suits or gowns designed by Adrian. She was married to John Gilbert from 1922 to 1924. Nils Asther (1897-1981) was a suave handsome leading man who was a film star in his native Sweden before coming to Hollywood in 1927. His silent films include *Topsy and Eva* (1927), *Sorrell and Son* (1927), and *Laugh, Clown, Laugh* (1928). His foreign accent impeded his success in sound movies. (1928)

Left:

In the Heart of the Berkshire Hills
Alice Joyce (1890-1955) was a beautiful leading lady in Vitagraph and Kalem silent movies, and appears on this cover as a youthful beauty representing Vitagraph pictures. She was a busy and popular actress from 1917-19 and starred in 17 silent films. Still playing ingénue parts in the 1920s, she made a smooth transition to more mature roles, eventually retiring in the early days of sound. (1918)

Romance
The Broadway hit play *Romance* was bought bag and baggage by D. W. Griffith, including the leading lady **Doris Keane** (1885-1945). Alas, the movie bombed and Griffith lost his shirt. The movie adaptation was said to be a turgid affair of a pastor in love with an opera singer who dallied with his old friend and is banished from him forever. English actor **Basil Sidney** (seen on cover with Miss Keane) played the priest. (1919) *Collection of James Nelson Brown*

The "Stone Face," Buster Keaton

Dreams, Just Dreams
Alice Joyce had a certain serenity and dignity that earned her the title "The Madonna of the Screen." Her memorable silent screen roles include the second Mrs. Dallas in the 1925 version of *Stella Dallas*, and Clara Bow's mother in *Dancing Mothers* in 1926. She was a model before entering movies, and posed for this beautiful song cover early in her film career. (1919)

She Doesn't
Buster Keaton (1895-1966) was an actor, director, producer, and screenwriter known as the "Stone Face" for his ability to project emotion with a minimum of facial expression. He played a homeless loser in the silent comedy *Go West* who leads a cattle drive with the help of his best friend, a baby cow called "Brown Eyes." Walter Winchell wrote the words, and Jimmie Durante and Chick Endor, the music, for this promotional song for the film. (1925) *Collection of Harold Jacobs*

141

Left:
It Must Be You
Buster Keaton started out as an acrobat in vaudeville and entered the movies in 1917. He made many silent comedy shorts and also feature length films, but few of his silent movies have theme songs. This song cover is from one of Keaton's first talking pictures made at M-G-M, *Free and Easy*. (1930) *Collection of James Nelson Brown*

Daughter of Mine
Madge Kennedy (1891-1987) was equally at home on stage or screen. As a gifted comedienne she co-starred on Broadway with W. C. Fields in the musical comedy *Poppy*, and also made many silent films for Samuel Goldwyn, including *Baby Mine* (1917), *The Service Star* (1918), and *The Girl with a Jazz Heart* (1921). She retired from the screen in the mid-1920s, but returned in the early 1950s playing character roles. (1919) *Collection of Harold Jacobs*

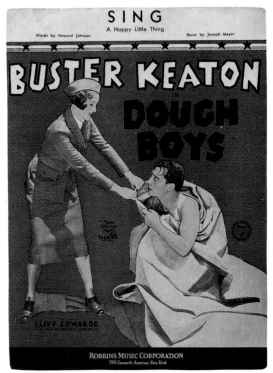

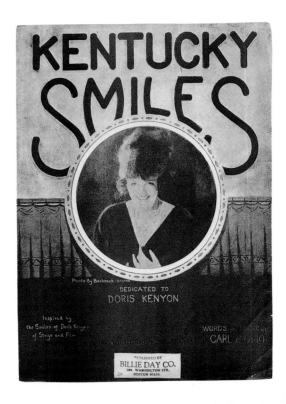

Right:
Kentucky Smiles
Doris Kenyon (1897-1979) started out in silent movies as an ingénue, but graduated to more mature roles in the 1920s culminating in the lead opposite Rudolph Valentino in *Monsieur Beaucaire*. This song, as stated on the cover, was "Inspired by the Smiles of Doris Kenyon of Stage and Film." (1920)

Sing
Buster Keaton spent some time as a doughboy in France with the 40th Infantry during the last months of World War I, and he built on his experiences in the all-talking picture *Dough Boys*, a comic romp featuring Keaton as a bumbling recruit. He appears with **Sally Eilers** on the song cover from the movie. Keaton is now considered by film historians a comic genius and a gifted director. (1930) *Collection of James Nelson Brown*

142

Left:

Just Because You Won My Heart

J. Warren Kerrigan (1879-1947) started his film career in 1909 as a Universal contract star, and he rose to great popularity playing dashing hero roles. He was a handsome screen personality who was dubbed "The Gibson Man." He appeared in dozens of silent movies, most notably *The Covered Wagon* (1923), until his retirement in 1924. (1916)

Poor Punchinello

Werner Krauss (1884-1959) was a German actor of some fame who appeared in more than 100 silent movies, a few of which were seen in the United States. Paramount Pictures released the Ufa German production of *Looping the Loop* starring Mr. Krauss as a sad circus clown who loses the girl to an acrobat. He is seen as mournful Punchinello on the cover of the movie theme song. Herr Krauss made several propaganda films for the Nazi regime during World War II and was made an Actor of the State. (1929)

Right:

Wrinkles

Alice Lake (1896-1967) is the little brunette lovely on the cover of this song. She started out in Mack Sennett comedies, graduating to leading lady parts with Metro Pictures. She made many silent movies in the 1920s, as well as a few talkies, but never attained real stardom. (1919)

The Flirt

Lydia Knott (1873-?) and **George Nichols** (1864-?) brought a certain maturity to their roles in the silent movie version of the Booth Tarkington story *The Flirt*, a small-town comedy drama produced by Universal-Jewel. Miss Knott had many 1920s silent movies to her credit, including *Blackmail*, *The Primrose Path* (1925 version), and *Our Dancing Daughters* (1928). Nichols also acted in many 1920s silent features including *The Barnstormer*, *Capital Punishment*, *White Gold*, and *The Wedding March*. (1923)

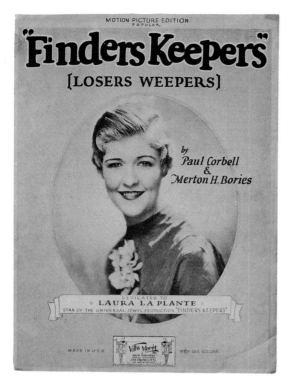

Finders Keepers
Laura La Plante (1904-1996) smiles from the cover of the title song from *Finders Keepers*. Miss La Plante was a vivacious comedienne at Universal-Jewel studios. She became one of their most preeminent stars during the 1920s, starring in Westerns, comedies, and melodramas. She played a beautiful blonde heroine in the 1927 silent version of *The Cat and the Canary*, and played the brunette Magnolia in the 1929 version of *Show Boat*. (1927)

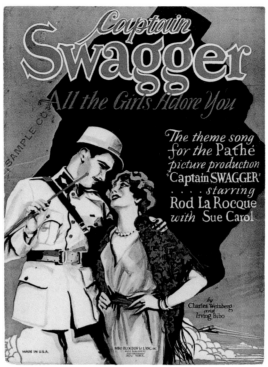

Captain Swagger
Rod La Rocque co-starred with **Sue Carol** in the Pathé silent movie production *Captain Swagger* that yielded this theme song. Mr. La Rocque made a smooth transition to talking movies, and he was active in films into the 1940s. After he retired he became a successful real estate broker. (1928)

Left:
Gigolo
Rod La Rocque (1896-1969) was a tall debonair leading man of the silents. He started his movie career with Essanay in 1914, later becoming a Cecil B. De Mille contract player. His marriage to Vilma Banky in 1927 was a celebrated affair, milked for all its worth by a publicity conscious studio. He appears here with **Jobyna Ralston** in a slinky dance scene in *Gigolo*. (1926)

Real Eyes
Lila Lee (1901-1973) was known as "Cuddles" in vaudeville with the Gus Edwards troupe. Her first movie was *The Cruise of the Make-Believe* in 1918, and she became a popular film star after appearing opposite Rudolph Valentino in *Blood and Sand* in 1922. She playing leading ladies in both silents and talkies until her retirement from the screen in 1937. (1919) *Collection of Harold Jacobs*

144

A Fire Laddie Just Like My Daddy
Ralph Lewis (1872-1937) started out in silents in 1914, and had a commanding screen presence. His strong performance as Austin Stoneman in D. W. Griffith's epic *Birth of a Nation* attracted critical praise. He was a solid, dependable actor through the years with a long list of screen credits including *Going Straight* and *Martha's Vindication* (1916), *Eyes of Youth* (1920), *Vengeance of the Deep* (1923), and *Dante's Inferno* (1924). He is seen as a fireman on this dramatic song cover from the FBO movie *The Third Alarm*. (1922) *Collection of Harold Jacobs*

For Heaven's Sake
Despite his bookish appearance **Harold Lloyd** was a daredevil athlete who thrilled audiences by performing his own zany stunts. In fact, he lost his right thumb and forefinger in a bad accident with a prop bomb during the filming of *Haunted Spooks* in 1920, and thereafter wore gloves in films to cover his handicap. His most famous stunt was in *Safety Last* (1923) where he scaled the side of a building and hung from a clock atop a skyscraper. This theme song is from his movie *For Heaven's Sake*, memorable for a chase scene through the city on a double-decker bus. (1926)

Left:
Girl Shy
Harold Lloyd (1893-1971) was one of the silent era's most popular comedians. He started out in a series of Hal Roach shorts, playing a character named Lonesome Luke who wore a small mustache like Charlie Chaplin's. It wasn't until he changed his image to an average-American bumbling youth with horn-rimmed glasses that he became a hit with audiences. He is now considered one of the greatest of silent screen comedians, and was awarded an honorary Oscar statuette in 1952 as "master comedian and good citizen." (1924)

Speedy Boy
Speedy was a great vehicle for **Harold Lloyd**'s talents. The story of a happy-go-lucky boy who couldn't keep a job for very long had Lloyd portraying a soda jerk, a Wall Street clerk, a Coney Island merrymaker, and a New York taxi driver. In one scene he drives his baseball idol, Babe Ruth, to Yankee Stadium. The climax of the movie is a wild cab drive down Fifth Avenue with attendant thrills. (1928)

145

Left:

One Little Smile
Bessie Love (1898-1986) was a D. W. Griffith discovery who matured from sweet girlish roles to serious leading lady roles during the 1920s. Her career peaked in 1929 when she showed her versatility by singing and dancing in the early M-G-M sound movie *The Broadway Melody*, earning an Academy Award nomination for best actress that subsequently went to Mary Pickford in *Coquette*. Her face was so familiar to the public that her name isn't even mentioned on this song cover. Miss Love later appeared on stage, screen, radio, and TV in England, working well into her seventies. (1930)

Charmaine (1927 edition)
This edition, published by Sherman, Clay & Company, is the more common of the two. Lew Pollack, now the proud lyricist, had his true name reinstated on the cover. The artistic rendering of the pretty French girl, Charmaine, represents Dolores del Rio who was the love interest of both Edmund Lowe and Victor McLaglen in *What Price Glory?* (1927)

Charmaine (1926 edition)
The movie *What Price Glory?* was patterned after Metro's successful *The Big Parade*. It too was set during World War I with spectacular battle scenes and a human interest love story. This first edition of the love theme from the movie was written with words by Louis Leazer and music by Erno Rapée, and published by Belwin. When the song became such a tremendous hit it was revealed that "Louis Leazer" was actually Lew Pollack who originally thought the song was a dud until it started making money. (1926) *Collection of Harold Jacobs*

So Dear to Me
Edmund Lowe (1890-1971) and **Victor McLaglen** (1886-1959) co-starred as Sergeant Quirk and Captain Flagg in *What Price Glory?*, and the combination was so effective that they continued to be cast together in other adventure films. *The Cock-Eyed World* was an early sound movie that starred the two, seen here on cover with Lili Damita. Lowe continued making films into the 1950s, as did McLaglen who crowned his career with an Academy Award for best actor in *The Informer* in 1935. (1929) *Collection of Harold Jacobs*

Left:
Sweet
Dorothy Mackaill (b. 1903) was a show girl from England who made a splash in the *Ziegfeld Follies* before going to Hollywood. She received the usual build-up from the studio including her photo on the cover of this popular song. She was equally at home in comedies or dramas, including the movies *The Fighting Blade* (1923), *Chickie* (1925), *Man Crazy* (1927), and *The Whip* (1928). Her career spanned the talkies, and she made several movies in the 1930s. (1921) *Collection of Harold Jacobs*

Daddy Mine
Mae Marsh (1895-1968), smiling sweetly from the cover of this World War I song, was one of D. W. Griffith's discoveries. She was considered by many to be the greatest dramatic actress of the silent era, by virtue of her moving roles as "The Little Sister" in *The Birth of a Nation*, and the grieving wife of Robert Harron in *Intolerance*. She did her best work under the guidance of Griffith including a memorable performance in *The White Rose* in 1923. Later work included occasional character roles in movies into the 1960s. (1918)

I'm a Cave Man
Shirley Mason (1901-1979) was the younger sister of silent screen actress Viola Dana. She started out in movies as a juvenile and played sweet romantic roles in more than ninety silent films until her retirement when sound movies took over. (1919)

Wait and See
Mary MacLaren (1896-1985) and **Jack Mulhall** (1887-1979) brighten the cover of this waltz ballad. Miss MacLaren was a Universal leading lady from about 1916 to 1924, and Mr. Mulhall was around for a long time, as a leading man during the silent era, and as a character actor in films into the 1950s. (1919)

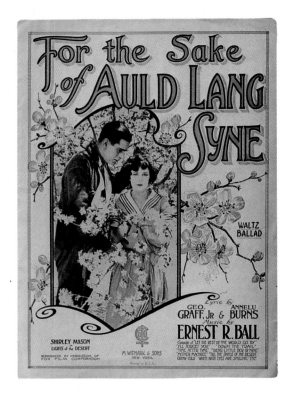

Left:
For the Sake of Auld Lang Syne
Shirley Mason appears on this sheet music cover with **Allan Forrest**, her co-star in the Fox silent movie *Lights of the Desert*. Miss Mason also starred in Mascot Studio's *Vultures of the Sea* (1928), a ten-chapter serial, with Johnnie Walker, Tom Santschi, and Boris Karloff. (1922)

Come Back to Me
Patsy Ruth Miller (b. 1905) worked in supporting roles until her big break as Esmeralda in the 1923 version of *The Hunchback of Notre Dame*. She played many more leading roles during the silent era, but her career faltered with the advent of sound, and she retired in 1931. She is seen here with co-star **Lawrence Gray** on the cover of a theme song from the Tiffany Stahl movie *Marriage by Contract*. (1927) *Collection of Harold Jacobs*

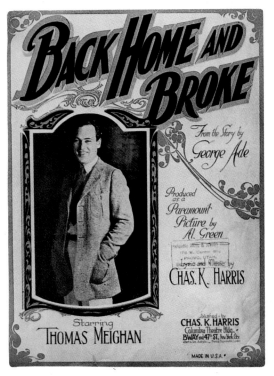

Right:
Anne of Green Gables
Mary Miles Minter (1902-1984) was the lovely actress who was implicated in the unsolved murder of silent film director William Desmond Taylor in 1922. Her career never recovered from the wild rumors circulating that her domineering stage mother, Charlotte Shelby, had killed Desmond. Miss Minter's photo is on the Barbelle cover of the theme song from *Anne of Green Gables*. (1919).

Back Home and Broke
Thomas Meighan (1879-1936) came to the movies from the stage. He typically portrayed strong, rugged, dependable hero types while under contract to Paramount from 1915-1928. His first big hit was in *The Miracle Man* (1919) with Lon Chaney. In *Back Home and Broke* he played a wealthy man pretending to be broke who secretly buys up most of his home town to exact retribution on townspeople who had earlier shunned him. Meighan continued to play leading men into the sound era. (1923)

Left:
Santa Fe
Tom Mix (1880-1940) was a real life adventurer, a soldier, a Western marshal, and a rodeo champion before he started making movies with the Selig Polyscope company in 1910. The colorful cover of this Williams and Van Alstyne song was designed by artist Starmer, and though uncredited, is thought to be an artistic rendering of Mr. Mix, the charismatic Western star of silent movies. (1910)

April Showers
Colleen Moore (1902-1988) and leading man, **Kenneth Harlan** (1895-1967) appear on the cover of the theme song from *April Showers*. Miss Moore started out in Hollywood as a star in B movies, often teamed with Tom Mix in Westerns. Mr. Harlan was a handsome matinee idol during the silent era who transcended the change to talkies and appeared in numerous films from 1917 to 1943. (1921)

Right:
Sally's In the Movies Now
Colleen Moore became highly popular in the 1920s cast as a fun-loving flapper type. She is seen here on the cover of a song from the First National silent movie production of the Ziegfeld musical comedy *Sally*. (1925)

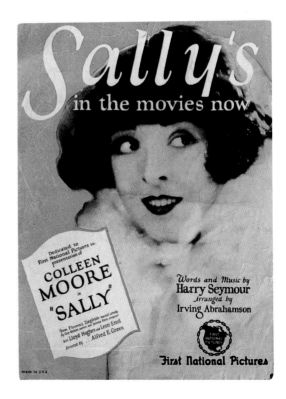

Tom Mix Fox Trot
Tom Mix's fast-paced action films were a big hit with both children and adults, and by 1920 he had become the most popular Western star in silent films. He made a slew of movies on into the 1930s, and also appeared with his famous horse Tony on tour with the Ringling Brothers Circus. (1919) *Collection of James Nelson Brown*

Left:
Jeannine I Dream of Lilac Time
Following the birth of sound movies, **Colleen Moore** starred in the silent film *Lilac Time*, playing a French girl who is mistakenly told at a military hospital that her lover, played by Gary Cooper, is dead. To accommodate the new passion for sound, the movie was issued in two versions—the silent version, to be shown with live orchestra, and the second, with recorded music and sound effects. (1928)

Heartsease
Tom Moore (1885-1955), Owen Moore's brother, is seen here with **Helene Chadwick** (1897-1940) on the cover of the theme song from *Heartsease*. Moore began his film career in 1908 at Biograph, and was a solid leading man for many years in silent movies. Miss Chadwick was a lovely leading lady of many romantic movies from the silents to the talkies. She died at age forty-two from serious injuries suffered in a fall. (1919)

Right:
Big Brother
Tom Moore played a reformed criminal in this silent movie adaptation of a Rex Beach story. He is seen here with child actor **Mickey Bennett** on the cover of the theme song from the Paramount movie *Big Brother*. (1923)

Piccadilly Jim
Owen Moore (1886-1939) and **Zena Keefe** (1896-1977) co-starred in the Selznick movie *Piccadilly Jim*. Mr. Moore, a handsome leading man type, starred in many of D. W. Griffith's early films, often playing lead to Mary Pickford whom he secretly married in 1910. Miss Keefe began as a young ingénue at Vitagraph from 1909-1916, moving to starring roles at Selznick in the late 'teens. Her movies include *Enlighten Thy Daughter* (1917), *After Midnight* (1921), and *The Broken Violin* (1923). She retired from films in 1924. (1919) *Collection of James Nelson Brown*

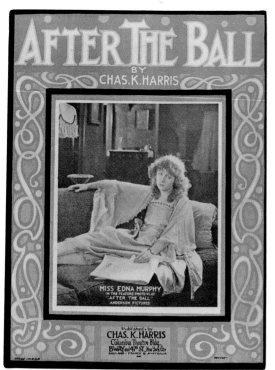

After the Ball
Edna Murphy (1899-1974) appeared in a long list of silent movies from 1919 through 1932 moving from ingénue to flapper roles. She is seen here on the cover of the theme song from the silent movie feature *After the Ball* by Anderson Pictures. (1924)

Right:
Jazzmania
At the peak of the Jazz Age, **Mae Murray** starred in the timely Tiffany production of *Jazzmania*. She was Tiffany's biggest box-office attraction during the 1920s starring in *The French Doll, Broadway Rose, Mademoiselle Midnight*, and *Fashion Row*. Tiffany silent productions earned some respect, but after the arrival of sound the studio took a new direction producing B movies and low-budget Westerns, eventually declining into obscurity. (1923) *Collection of James Nelson Brown*

Fascination
Mae Murray (1885-1965) was a gifted dancer with Vernon Castle on Broadway, later becoming a *Ziegfeld Follies* regular. She made her first movie in 1916, and became a popular star of the silent era. She enjoyed her fame, and rode around in her chauffeur-driven Rolls-Royce snuggled under a luxurious sable lap robe. Her personality and good looks were said to be greater than her acting ability, and her career took a downward turn shortly after the sound revolution. She is seen here on the cover of the title song from the Metro production of *Fascination*. (1922)

Oh Louella!
Carmel Myers (1899-1980) started in films at Triangle studios under the tutelage of D. W. Griffith, and later starred opposite such famous leading men as Rudolph Valentino and John Barrymore. She was never a major star, and retired from films in the early 1930s, returning sporadically to play character roles. She wrote the words and music for this song. (1927)

Left:
A Connecticut Yankee
Harry C. Myers (1882-1938) was a leading man in both silents and early talkies. He is probably best known as the drunken millionaire in Charlie Chaplin's *City Lights* (1931). He played the title role in *A Connecticut Yankee at King Arthur's Court*, and appears in a ridiculous getup on the theme song cover. (1922)

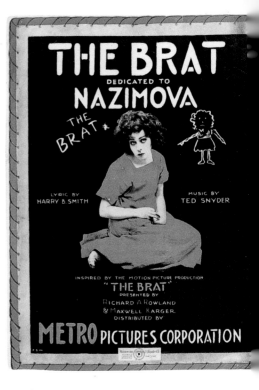

The Brat
Alla Nazimova (1879-1945), usually referred to simply as Nazimova, was a talented Russian actress drafted from the Broadway stage into silent movies. Her first picture was the antiwar *War Brides* in which her effective acting won critical praise. She is seen here on the cover of the title song from Metro Pictures' silent movie *The Brat*. (1919)

Alla
This beautiful art cover of **Alla Nazimova** adorns a song written by Anita Owen inscribed, "Admiringly dedicated to the famous artiste and Metro star Mme. Alla Nazimova." Nazimova was respected and admired, but perhaps became too "arty" for her audiences, and she retired from the screen in 1925, reappearing later as a character actress in a few 1940s movies. (1920)

Nanook
Robert Flaherty was the creator of the history-making *Nanook of the North*, the first popular feature-length documentary. While on an exploratory expedition, he became interested in filming the life of the Eskimo and his fight for existence. As his subject, he chose **Nanook**, a famous hunter of the Far North, and made an extraordinary biographical film of him and his family as they lived for a year. Footage included a daring seal-hunt and a brave struggle with a walrus, as well as the everyday activities of an Eskimo family. The film was a huge financial and critical success, admired to this day. (1922) *Collection of Harold Jacobs*

Left:

The Red Lantern

This theme song from Metro Pictures' production *The Red Lantern* shows the gifted silent screen star **Nazimova** in full costume and head gear. She produced other prestigious silent movies in which she also starred including *Camille* in 1921, *A Doll's House* in 1922, and *Salome* in 1923. (1919)

The Beggar

From 1923 to 1929 **Pola Negri** was one of the foremost stars of the silent screen, bringing to the screen a certain exoticism and glamour that found favor with audiences for a time. In *The Secret Hour* she played a mail order bride who is torn between a vineyard owner and his young foreman. She appears on the cover of this theme song from the Paramount silent production. (1927)

The Spanish Dancer

Pola Negri (1894-1987) was born in Poland and started out in German films, later becoming a Hollywood star. *Bella Donna* was her first U. S. movie, and she was accorded the full star build-up by Paramount, much to the chagrin of Gloria Swanson, the reigning queen of the lot. Miss Negri appears on the cover of the theme song from *The Spanish Dancer*, a romantic drama set in old Spain. (1923)

Sunbeams Bring Dreams of You Loves of an Actress was one of the last silent movies **Pola Negri** made in the United States. She is seen on cover with co-star **Nils Asther**. Her type of earthy, exotic beauty began to pall with audiences towards the end of the 1920s, and her thick foreign accent precluded her success in talking pictures in the United States, and she returned to Europe in 1929. Her fascinating personal life had her romantically linked at various times with Valentino and Adolf Hitler, and married first to a count, then a prince. (1928)

THE RIVER'S END
WORDS & MUSIC BY HARRY HOCH & ARTHUR BEHIM

DEDICATED TO MARSHALL A. NEILAN, THE YOUNGEST DIRECTOR-GENIUS OF MOTION PICTURES, ON THE OCCASION OF HIS FIRST INDEPENDENT PRODUCTION OF THE SAME TITLE BY JAMES OLIVER CURWOOD, WHICH HAS INSPIRED THIS OFFERING.

Left:
The River's End
Marshall Neilan (1891-1958) was D. W. Griffith's chauffeur before he tried his hand at acting. He starred in many silent productions as a handsome leading man, and also wrote occasional screenplays, winding up as a prominent director with many fine movies to his credit. A drinking problem eventually took its toll, and his career fell into decline. His brilliant directing of the film adaptation of James Oliver Curwood's *The River's End* inspired this musical dedication with his photo on cover. (1920)

Why Didn't You Leave Me Years Ago
INSTEAD OF LEAVING ME NOW

MABEL NORMAND
Goldwyn Pictures

Words by
SIDNEY D. MITCHELL
& GRANT CLARKE

Music by
ARCHIE GOTTLER

Why Didn't You Leave Me Years Ago
Mabel Normand (1894-1930) was a Mack Sennett leading lady, and a talented comedienne at Keystone studios for many years, suffering anything for a laugh including being tied to the railroad tracks, dragged through a muddy lake, and plastered with countless custard pies. After her big hit in the Mack Sennett movie *Mickey*, Miss Normand was looking for greener pastures, and she left Sennett's company for a five-year contract with Goldwyn Pictures. She appears on this sparkling cover under the auspices of her new boss. (1920)

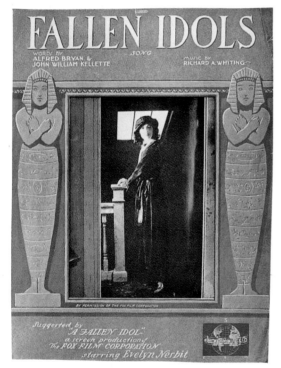

FALLEN IDOLS
SONG
Words by
ALFRED BRYAN &
JOHN WILLIAM KELLETTE
Music by
RICHARD A. WHITING

BY PERMISSION OF THE FOX FILM CORPORATION

Suggested by
"A FALLEN IDOL"
a screen production of
The FOX FILM CORPORATION
starring Evelyn Nesbit

Fallen Idols
Evelyn Nesbit (1885-1967), of the notorious Stanford White murder trial, was an ambitious beauty who continued her show business career even after her husband Henry Thaw was imprisoned. She only made two silent movies—*The Hidden Woman* in 1922 and the Fox movie *A Fallen Idol*. Lovely Miss Nesbit smiles from the cover of this theme song. (1919)

OH! MABEL, BEHAVE

MABEL NORMAND

by
CLIFF FRIEND
AND
IRVIN G. HUP

JACK MILLS INC.

PRINTED IN U.S.A.

Oh! Mabel, Behave
Mabel Normand was cast with Owen Moore in the Mack Sennett comedy *Oh! Mabel, Behave*. She should have taken the advice in the song title, as her private life was falling apart. She started giving wild parties and showing up late for work or not at all, and gossip linked her to drug addiction. (1922)
Collection of Harold Jacobs

154

Left:

Suzanna [bride picture]
More ugly rumors surfaced during the investigation of the lurid murder of studio executive, handsome William Desmond Taylor. When Taylor was shot to death in his Hollywood mansion, the inquest revealed that he was involved with both **Mabel Normand** and Mary Miles Minter, and that both women had visited him on the night of the shooting. Though proven innocent of the crime, her name was publicly linked to drug use and her reputation was tarnished beyond repair. *Suzanna* was one of her last feature films. (1923)

Midshipman
Ramon Novarro (1899-1968) was a romantic lead in the 1920s, rivaling Valentino as a Latin lover. His best known part was the title role in *Ben Hur* in 1926. In *The Midshipman* he played an undergraduate at the US Naval Academy, enduring rigorous authentic training sequences. Much of the exterior shooting was done at Annapolis, and this fine pictorial song cover shows scenes from the movie. (1925) *Collection of Harold Jacobs*

Suzanna [in sombrero]
Despite its publication in two cover versions, the theme song from **Mabel Normand**'s movie *Suzanna* failed to help her damaged image, and the movie was withdrawn after it was boycotted by an unfriendly public. A second scandal involving her chauffeur who was found standing over the body of Hollywood millionaire Cortland S. Dines holding a pistol belonging to Mabel was the final blow to her reputation. Mabel Normand died at age thirty-six from a combination of tuberculosis and pneumonia. (1923)

You're the Only One for Me
The Flying Fleet had some synchronized sound effects and music, but no dialogue. **Ramon Novarro** was a flyer in this Navy film that included actual flight sequences with the help of the United States Naval Academy's flying school. He is seen with **Anita Page** on the cover of this theme song. Novarro ended up another victim of Hollywood tragedy. On a Halloween night in 1968, intruders burst into his home in the Hollywood Hills and beat him to death. (1929)

Left:
The Perfect Lover
Eugene O'Brien (1882-1966) emotes with **Lucille Stewart** on the cover of the theme song from the Selznick picture *The Perfect Lover*. O'Brien was a Broadway actor before embarking on his film career, in which he frequently starred opposite Norma Talmadge with whom he had a special screen rapport. (1919)

The Shepherd of the Hills
Molly O'Day (1911-) started out as a leading lady in Hal Roach comedies in the early 1920s, moving on to better roles in late silents and early talkies. She appears on the cover of the theme song from the silent movie adaptation of Harold Bell Wright's book *The Shepherd of the Hills*. Her career met an inglorious end when she became excessively obese. (1927)

Right:
Mike
Sally O'Neill (1908-1968) was Molly O'Day's sister. She was a petite leading lady who frequently played street urchin roles as seen on this cover promoting the Marshall Neilan comedy *Mike*. She made many movies, both silent and sound, until her career tapered off in the 1930s. (1926)

Fires of Faith
The Famous Players-Lasky production of *Fires of Faith* starred **Eugene O'Brien** and **Catherine Calvert**, seen on the cover of the theme song in a touching scene from the movie. The song was dedicated to the spunky Salvation Army evangelist, Commander Evangeline Booth. (1919)

Left:
Stay in Your Own Backyard
Hal Roach launched the *Our Gang* comedies in 1922, a series about the escapades of an engaging troupe of children who charmed the public for over twenty years. This early cover from the movie *Your Own Back Yard* shows some of the original cast that continually changed through the years. Identified are chubby Joe Cobb, far right, with freckle-faced Mickey Daniels next to him, and Mary Kornman, far left. The little black child, Farina, played by Allen Clayton Hoskins, appears in the foreground. Hal Roach said "...they talked and acted exactly like children really do. And that's what made *Our Gang* so popular." (1925) *Collection of Harold Jacobs*

Himalya
Olga Petrova (1886-1977) was born Muriel Harding, but she took the more exotic show business name to ride the wave of popularity of foreign "vamp" types like Theda Bara and Pola Negri. Even to her friends who knew better she insisted on being addressed as Madame Petrova. She did well for a few years playing femme fatale parts, then went into the production end of movies, and also did some script writing. (1919)

On the Lagoon
Virginia Pearson (1888-1958) was frequently cast in exotic vampire roles, including the part of Carlotta with Lon Chaney in the 1925 version of *The Phantom of the Opera*. She appeared in many other silent movies including 1914's *The Actress* to 1925's Chadwick production of *The Wizard of Oz* in which she appeared with Oliver Hardy. She is seen here in a typical exotic pose. (1920)

Right:
Surrender
Lovely **Mary Philbin** (b. 1903) was a former beauty queen who worked in films from 1921 to 1929 when talkies took over. Her most memorable role was Christine, the heroine in the 1925 version of *Phantom of the Opera*. This theme song is from one of her last movies, the Universal-Jewel silent movie *Surrender*. (1927) *Collection of Harold Jacobs*

The Right to Happiness
Dorothy Phillips (1892-1980) was a fine dramatic actress who starred in Universal silent movies in the 'teens. She is frequently seen on sheet music covers, this one from the movie *The Right to Happiness*, and others from *Destiny*, *Once to Every Woman*, and *The Heart of Humanity*. (1919)

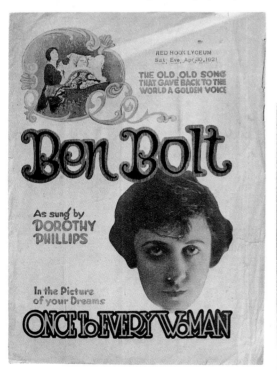

Ben Bolt
Dorothy Phillips starred in the Universal-Jewel production of *Once to Every Woman*, a melodramatic story about an opera singer. Margaret Mann played the sympathetic mother role in the movie, and appears on the back cover of the song sheet. (1920)

Sweetheart of Mine
Mary Pickford (1893-1979) started her film career in 1909 with D. W. Griffith at Biograph studio. At first, she was not identified by name as was the custom in the early days of film-making. But before long everyone knew that the radiant screen personality with the golden curls was Mary Pickford. This official Mary Pickford song has her facsimile signature. (1914)

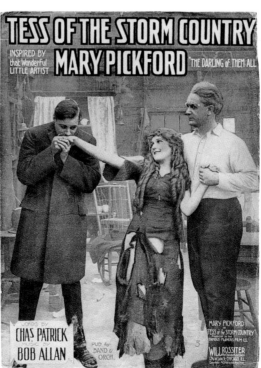

Tess of the Storm Country
Mary Pickford was paid $500 a week when she made *Tess of the Storm Country* for Famous Players. It established her as a major star with a salary increase to $2,000 a week and half the profits on her productions. She was quite a little businesswoman and by mid-1916 had a contract for $10,000 weekly, a $300,000 bonus, and a share in the profits of the studio! Other cover stars are **Harold Lockwood** (left) and **Jean Hersholt** (right). (1915)

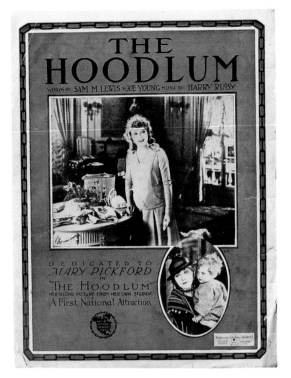

Left:

The Hoodlum

When her contract with Famous Players expired in 1918, **Mary Pickford** became her own producer, releasing her films through First National. She is seen here on the cover of the theme song from *The Hoodlum* in which she played the role of little Amy Burke. This was her second picture from her own studio. (1919)

Love Has a Way

As a partner in the United Artists Corporation **Mary Pickford** starred in *Dorothy Vernon of Haddon Hall*, a historical romance in which she played a grown-up 18-year old English aristocrat wearing elegant period costumes. Though the movie was a profitable venture, her public was less than enthralled and wanted their sweet little girl back. (1924)

Dear Old Daddy Long Legs

Mary Pickford was dubbed "America's Sweetheart." In most of her films she portrayed a sweet, innocent, lovable little girl. Her charm, dimpled good looks, golden curls, and childlike appeal combined to make her the nation's biggest box-office draw. She poses on the cover of the theme song for *Daddy Long Legs*, with an inset photo of her as the sprightly lass, Judy Adams, whom she portrayed in the film. (1919)

I'll Tell the World

This lovely collectible song by Harold B. Freeman has a colorful cover drawing by Leo Sielkeur that captures the charm and innocence of **Mary Pickford**. (1919)

Left:
Little Annie Rooney
Mary Pickford brought back her long golden curls, short frocks, and mischievous dirty face, again playing a child in *Little Annie Rooney*. Though she was now thirty-two, her portrayal was sincere and believable, and a delighted public flocked to see the movie. (1925)

★ ★ ★ ★ ★

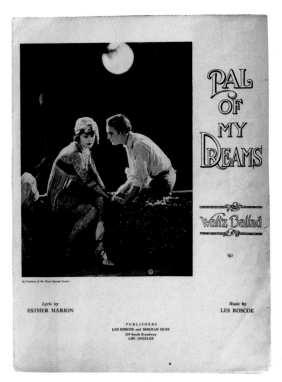

Pal of My Dreams
Marie Prevost (1898-1937) is seen with **George O'Hara** on the cover of this waltz ballad. Miss Prevost was originally a Mack Sennett Bathing Beauty, but proved her acting ability and was soon cast in leading lady roles. She reached stardom playing romantic comedy roles. Her career ended in the mid-1930s when she started to have a problem with her weight. Crash dieting didn't help, and she developed an eating disorder that eventually led to her death from malnutrition at age thirty-eight. (1920)

Right:
The Valley of the Giants
Wallace Reid (1891-1923) was a handsome leading man, and a major star in silent films, whose narcotics related death shocked the nation. He was addicted to morphine, probably administered as the result of an earlier accident. Following on the heels of the William Desmond Taylor murder and the Fatty Arbuckle case, this scandal led to the formation of the Hays office to regulate the morals, not only of movies, but also of movie stars. Mr. Reid co-starred with **Grace Darmond** (1898-1963) in *The Valley of the Giants*, an outdoor adventure drama based on a novel by Peter Kyne. (1919) *Collection of Harold Jacobs*

The Fire Brigade
Charles Ray (1891-1943) entered movies from the stage, and was typically typecast as a country boy who manages to surmount his humble beginnings to win the girl at the end of the movie. He played a fireman in M-G-M's *The Fire Brigade* in love with **May McAvoy** (b. 1901), the daughter of a crooked politician whose reckless approval of shoddy building contracts results in disaster. Miss McAvoy also starred in *The Enchanted Cottage* (1924) *Lady Windemere's Fan* (1925), *Ben Hur* (1926), and *The Jazz Singer* (1927). (1926) *Collection of Harold Jacobs*

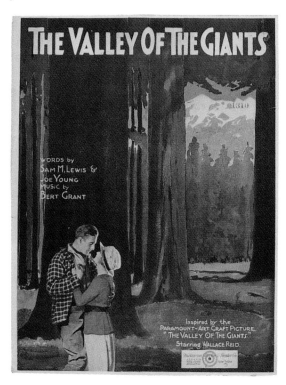

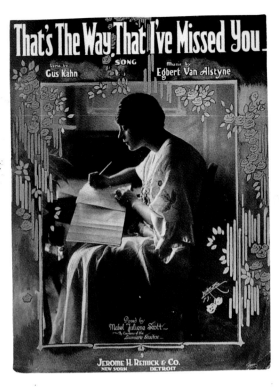

Left:

Mothers of Men
This silent movie theme song was written in conjunction with the photoplay *Mothers of Men*, a World War I production of the **Robards Players**. The dramatic cover drawing by E. E. Walton shows wraith-like visions of Washington, Lincoln, and President Wilson emerging from the smoke. The lyrics praise the mothers of the men who go to fight the foe. (1917)

That's the Way that I've Missed You
Mabel Juliene Scott was an active actress in the 1920s. One of her better known roles was Reginald Denny's leading lady in Universal's *The Abysmal Brute* (1923), the story of a society girl and a backwoods prizefighter. Other movies include the 1920 version of *The Sea Wolf*, *Behold My Wife* (1921), and *The Power of a Lie* (1922), a brother-sister drama co-starring David Torrence. (1919)

Right:

A Yankee Doodle in Berlin
Mack Sennett (1880-1960) began as an actor with American Biograph, but by 1912 had established his own production unit, the Keystone Company. Within a year his slapstick "pie-in-the-face" Keystone Cop comedies were famous, earning for him the title "King of Laughter." Sennett's famous Studio Bathing Girls, including luscious Phyllis Haver (top row, far right), appear on the cover of the theme song from *Yankee Doodle in Berlin*, a World War I comedy with Ben Turpin playing a cross-eyed Kaiser. (1919)

The Garden of Allah
Thomas Santschi (1880-1931) and **Helen Ware** (1877-1939) co-starred in *The Garden of Allah*, a Selig movie based on a 1904 novel by Robert Hichens. Provocative movie scenes and photos of the two stars on the cover of the theme song helped to draw audiences to the theaters. Santschi was a leading man of the early 'teens with Selig studios, appearing in the serial *The Adventures of Kathlyn*. Helen Ware starred in 1920s movies, including the role of Ma Taylor in *The Virginian* (1929). She continued her stage career while making movies. (1917)

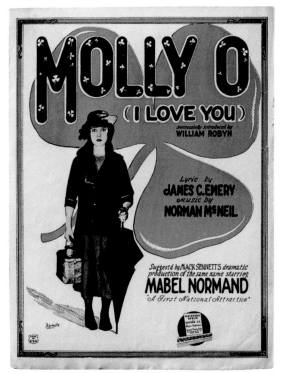

The Valley of Content
Norma Shearer (1900-1983) started out in silent features in 1920, and rose to stardom while married to Irving Thalberg, a top M-G-M studio boss who aided her career. She eventually won an Academy Award for her performance in *The Divorcee* (1930). Though most famous for her sound movies such as *Marie Antoinette* (1936) and *Romeo and Juliet* (1938), she made many silent films, and is seen here with **Huntley Gordon** in a scene from the Louis B. Mayer silent screen production *Pleasure Mad*. (1923)

Molly O
Mack Sennett cared deeply for his wide-eyed luminous star, **Mabel Normand**, and once described her as being "as beautiful as a spring morning." She appears on the cover of the theme song from the Sennett dramatic production *Molly O* (1921)

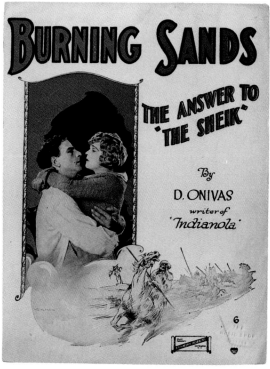

Burning Sands
Milton Sills (1882-1930) came to Hollywood in 1914 with a solid stage background, and was a dependable leading man in many silent films to the birth of the talkies. He appeared in a wide range of movies from period swashbucklers to comedies and melodramas. With his good speaking voice, he was slated to move smoothly into talkies until his premature death at age forty-eight from a heart attack. *Burning Sands* co-starred him with **Wanda Hawley**, both on the cover of the movie theme song. (1922)

Help! Help! Mr. Sennett
Mack Sennett appears on this song cover with more of his beautiful Bathing Girls. His autobiography *King of Comedy* (Doubleday, 1954) gives an illuminating insider's view of his world of comedy. (1919) *Collection of Harold Jacobs*

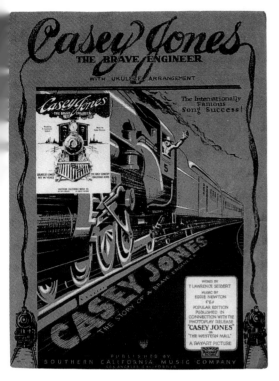

Mary Regan
Anita Stewart was an established star at Vitagraph in 1917 when she left to head her own movie company with Louis B. Mayer as production executive. The beautiful Miss Stewart achieved even greater heights under his guidance. *Mary Regan*, based on a novel by LeRoy Scott, starred her in the title role. Also a talented songwriter, Miss Stewart composed this song as well as many other theme songs for her movies. (1919)

Casey Jones
The Rayart Picture company, founded in 1924 by W. Ray Johnston of later Monogram fame, produced *Casey Jones or The Western Mail*, the story of the legendary brave engineer co-starring veteran film player **Al St. John** (1893-1963) and Ralph Lewis. Rayart Pictures produced many silent serials during the late 1920s before restructuring in 1930 as Monogram. (1927)

At Close of Day
Lewis Stone's (1879-1953) acting career was interrupted by service as a major in the cavalry during World War I. After the Armistice he developed into a solid, dependable actor in *The Prisoner of Zenda* (1922), *Scaramouche* (1923), and *The Lost World* (1925). He garnered an Academy Award nomination for best actor in *The Patriot* (1928), but he lost out to Warner Baxter. In the 1940s he moved into character parts, most memorable as Judge Hardy in the Andy Hardy movies at M-G-M. He appears with **Peggy Wood** on the cover of the part-talkie *Wonder of Women* in which he played a composer torn between two women. (1929)

Because You Believe in Me
Anita Stewart (1895-1961) entered films with Vitagraph in 1911, and she and **Earle Williams** (1880-1927) were frequently co-starred as Vitagraph's reigning romantic couple. They played the lovers Celestia and Tommy Barclay in Vitagraph's 1915 serial *The Goddess*. Mr. Williams was an active leading man at Vitagraph, and made scores of silent movies from 1908 until his death in 1927. (1918)

Left:
Answering Eyes
Bluebeard's Eighth Wife was a sophisticated comedy based on a hit Broadway play. **Gloria Swanson** (1897-1983) played a French society girl who, after marrying a rich American, is outraged to find she is his eighth wife. **Huntley Gordon** (1897-1956) played the oft-married husband who must prove his sincerity and undying devotion to Swanson before she will consummate the marriage. The two stars appear on the cover of an English printing of the movie song. (1926) *Collection of James Nelson Brown*

The Hushed Hour
Blanche Sweet (1895-1986) was a major dramatic star with D. W. Griffith, playing the title roles in two of his landmark productions—*The Lonedale Operator* (1911) in which she portrayed a brave telegraph operator who helps thwart a gang of payroll bandits, and *Judith of Bethulia* (1914). She is seen here on the cover of the theme song from the Harry Garson silent movie *The Hushed Hour*. (1919)

The Talmadge Sisters, Constance and Norma

The Love Waltz
This theme song for *The Love of Sunya* was inspired by glamorous **Gloria Swanson**. The movie, financed by Joseph Kennedy, father of the future president, was the opening feature at the fabulous new Roxy Theater. Miss Swanson began her movie career making light comedies at Mack Sennett's Keystone company. She later became a top star in such melodramas as *Teddy at the Throttle* in which she was tied to the railroad tracks by Wallace Beery, the villain, who was also her first husband. (1927)

Temp'rament
Constance Talmadge (1900-1973), the youngest of the three Talmadge sisters, found her acting niche in sophisticated comedies for which she had a decided flair. 1919 was a big year for her. Not only was she featured in D. W. Griffith's *The Fall of Babylon*, she also starred in *A Temperamental Wife*, seen here with co-star **Wyndham Standing** on a song cover from the movie. (1919) *Collection of Harold Jacobs*

I Wonder
Constance Talmadge never reached the pinnacle of success that her sister Norma enjoyed, but they were never competitors as their talents lay in different areas. Norma's forte was the melodrama, and Constance was more entertaining in lighter roles. She retired from films without making a single talkie. Miss Talmadge is the artistic subject of this lovely pastel cover on a song by Irving Berlin. (1919) *Collection of Harold Jacobs*

Norma Fox Trot
Norma Talmadge was only fourteen when she made her debut as a leading lady in the first screen version of *A Tale of Two Cities*. In 1917 she married motion picture mogul Joseph Schenck, twenty years her senior, and under his shrewd management rose to super stardom in the 1920s. This fox trot song was named for her, and she appears on the cover in a dramatic posture reminiscent of the oft-quoted line by the fictional Norma Desmond in *Sunset Boulevard*, "I'm ready for my close-up, Mr. De Mille." (1920)

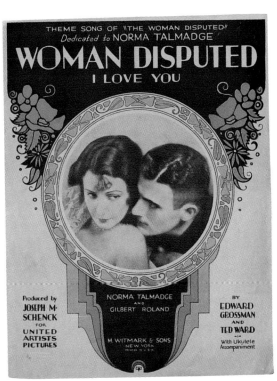

The New Moon
Norma Talmadge (1897-1957) was the most famous of the three acting Talmadge sisters. Constance Talmadge was a respected actress in her own right, while Natalie met with less success with only two feature films in the 1920s and was better known as Buster Keaton's wife. Norma was a fine dramatic actress, a major silent film star who was at her best portraying tragic long-suffering heroines. She is seen here on the cover of an Irving Berlin theme song composed for *The New Moon*. (1919)

Woman Disputed, I Love You
Norma Talmadge was a top box office draw, and made over 250 movies before her retirement in 1945. *The Woman Disputed* was her last silent film in which she co-starred with **Gilbert Roland**, the two of them seen on this cover. When talking pictures became the rage in Hollywood, Miss Talmadge was obliged to take diction lessons to try to disguise her Brooklyn accent before she could make her first talkie, *New York Nights*. Despite the lessons and the support of her handsome co-star Gilbert Roland, she was unsuccessful coping with the demands of sound, and soon retired from the screen completely. (1928)

165

Left:
West of the Great Divide
Alice Terry (1901-1987) and
Conway Tearle (1878-1938) appear
on the theme song cover from Metro
Goldwyn's silent movie *The Great
Divide*. Miss Terry was an elegant
blonde who co-starred with romantic
leading men like Rudolf Valentino in
The Four Horsemen of the Apocalypse,
and Ramon Novarro in *The Prisoner of
Zenda*. In *The Great Divide* she is
rescued from the clutches of lecherous
Wallace Beery by the hero Conway
Tearle, a distinguished silent star
usually cast in hero roles. (1924)

Lenore
Lenore Ulrich (1892-1970) was both a stage and
screen actress billed as "the magic mistress of a
thousand emotions." As the protégée of stage
impresario David Belasco she became an important
Broadway star. One of her greatest theatrical
successes was *Tiger Rose*, which she later made as a
silent movie in 1923. Other Ulrich song covers are
from the films *The Heart of Paula* (1916), *Frozen
Justice* (1929), and *South Sea Rose* (1929). This song
with a vibrant color cover by Manning was dedicated
to Miss Ulrich. (1921) *Collection of Harold Jacobs*

Below:
Just for a While
Olive Thomas (1898-1920) was raised in poverty, and
was trapped in a teen-age marriage before she broke away
and worked her way up the ladder of success. She was a
Ziegfeld Follies' showgirl and a photographers' model for
the magazines *Vogue* and *Vanity Fair* before entering
movies. When she married Jack Pickford, Mary's brother,
she appeared to be a young lady who had everything. But
appearances were deceptive, for tragedy stalked her. After a
night on the town in Paris, she apparently swallowed some
poisonous pills by mistake, thinking they were sleeping
pills, and died a painful lingering death. (1920)

☆ ☆ ☆ ☆ ☆
The Sheik, Rudolph Valentino

Right:
I Have a Rendezvous with You
Rudolph Valentino (1895-1926)
was a handsome Latin-lover sex symbol
of the 1920s who became a legend after
his premature death. In his first movie
The Four Horsemen of the Apocalypse,
he played a tango dancer, and was an
instant sensation. He is seen here with
Alice Terry on the dramatic song
cover, flanked by the four apocalyptic
heads—Conquest, Famine, War, and
Death. *The Sheik*, also made in 1921,
found Valentino firmly enthroned as the
idol of millions of women. (1921)
Collection of Roy Bishop

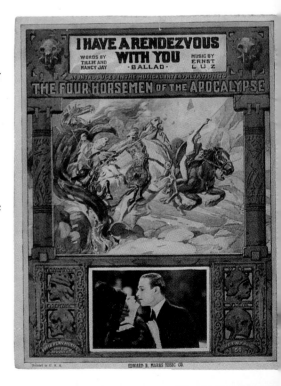

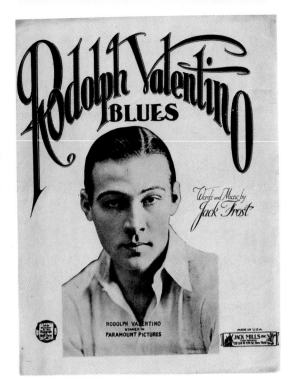

Right:
Rodolph Valentino Blues
Comic blues song tells of fictional Mary Brown who turns down all the village fellows because she has a crush on movie star **Rudolph Valentino** (real name, Rodolfo Guglielmi). She sighs, "...You've got a way of making love... that Wally Reid knows nothing of..." This same photo was used after Valentino's death on the song cover "There's a New Star in Heaven Tonight." (1922)

You Gave Me Your Heart (#1)
The Paramount silent movie *Blood and Sand* starred **Valentino** as a glamorous young matador who risks everything—his career, his marriage, even his life—while under the spell of a voluptuous seductress, played by Nita Naldi. This too was a box-office hit. (1922)

Left:
You Gave Me Your Heart (#2)
Valentino's photo on the cover sold a lot of sheet music, and the theme song from *Blood and Sand* was so popular, it had this alternate cover designed by Frederick S. Manning. **Lila Lee**, shown here with **Valentino**, played his wife in the movie, forbearing his infidelity, and standing by faithfully as the tragedy unfolds. (1922)

Red Red Rose
The cover of this love theme from Paramount's *Monsieur Beaucaire* shows a foppish **Valentino** in period costume kissing co-star **Doris Kenyon**. His rather effeminate screen image was due to the pressures of his misguided second wife, Natacha Rambova, who took charge of his costume and make-up with disastrous results. A *Chicago Tribune* editorial ridiculed Valentino as a "Pink Powder Puff," leading to a strongly worded reply by an outraged Valentino challenging the journalist to a duel in a boxing or wrestling arena. The challenge went unanswered. (1924)

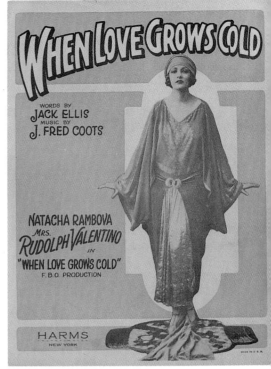

Left:
Son of the Sheik
Valentino's last movie, *Son of the Sheik*, was thought by many to be his best. It was a sequel to *The Sheik*, and he still had that special sensuality and charisma that drove women crazy. **Vilma Banky** played the nomadic dancing girl *Yasmin* who, after numerous travails, rides off with him on his dashing steed to his sheikdom. Valentino's death on the eve of the film's release led to a huge surge at the box-office and enormous profits for United Artists studio. (1926) ✓ *Collection of Harold Jacobs*

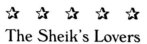

The Sheik's Lovers

When Love Grows Cold
Natacha Rambova (1897-1966) was actually Winifred Shaunessy Hudnut, the stepdaughter of Richard Hudnut, the millionaire cosmetic king. She took her exotic name while dancing in a European ballet troupe. She and Valentino were married in Mexico in 1922 in a union that lasted only three years. She appeared in but one feature film, *When Love Grows Cold*, forebodingly on the eve of their separation. She was in France when he died. (1926) *Collection of Harold Jacobs*

We Will Meet at the End of the Trail
Jean Acker (1893-1978) rose from obscurity as Valentino's first wife. She reportedly locked him out of their bridal suite on their wedding night leaving the marriage unconsummated. She had an unspectacular career in movies despite her connection to Valentino. Miss Acker composed this maudlin tribute to Valentino with a prominent cover photo of herself. She may have waited at the end of the trail, but it is unlikely that he did. (1926) ✓

Montmartre
Widespread shock and hysteria swept through Valentino's legion of female fans when he died at age thirty-one from post-operative complications due to a perforated ulcer and ruptured appendix. **Pola Negri**'s name was linked romantically to Valentino's, and in typical Hollywood fashion, she collapsed beside his coffin at the funeral home. Valentino fan clubs continued to blossom even after his death, and his mystique grew when each year on the anniversary of his death a mysterious woman in black laid flowers on his grave, adding to the legend of the handsome young star. (1924)

Left:
You Know How 'Tis!
Virginia Valli (1895-1968) was a beautiful brunette contract star for Universal studios in the 1920s who rose to stardom in *The Storm*, a dramatic silent movie whose high point was a massive forest fire. She made many other silent melodramas including *The Pleasure Garden* (1925), Alfred Hitchcock's first feature. She retired in 1931 after marrying actor Charles Farrell. (1922)

The Land of Broken Dreams
Florence Vidor (1895-1977) was active in silent movies from 1916 to 1929, equally at home in dramas or comedies. Some of her credits include *A Tale of Two Cities* (1915), *Hail the Woman* (1921), *Alice Adams* (1923), *Barbara Frietchie* (title role, 1924), and her last film *Chinatown Nights* (1929). She was first married to director King Vidor, later divorced him, and married violinist Jascha Heifetz. Her career came to an abrupt halt when her voice was found to be unsuitable for talking pictures. (1923)

Give Your Little Baby Lots of Lovin'!
Lupe Velez (1908-1944) was a tempestuous Latin type who broke into movies towards the end of the silent era. Her first big break was opposite Douglas Fairbanks in *The Gaucho*, followed by other typical roles as a fiery hot-blooded woman. Her personal life was full of turmoil with a much-publicized volatile marriage to Johnny Weismuller that ended in divorce, and a series of unsuccessful love affairs. Pregnant and unmarried, she killed herself by swallowing pills, but only after meticulous preparation of her hair and makeup. (1928) *Collection of Harold Jacobs*

Told in the Hills
Robert Warwick (1878-1964) trained for an operatic career, but was lured instead into the movies. He was a dependable and stalwart leading man in silents, then moved smoothly into the world of talkies as a character actor. He is seen here with co-star Ann Little on the cover of the theme song for Paramount's backwoods drama *Told in the Hills*. **Ann Little** (1894-1984) was the unsung heroine in several 15-chapter serial films of the 1920s, and always the recipient of good notices—*Lightning Bryce* (1919), *The Blue Fox* (1921), *Nan of the North* (1922), *The Eagle's Talons* (1923), and *Secret Service Saunders* (1925). *Collection of Harold Jacobs*

169

Oh! Susanna
Lois Wilson (1898-1988) was a Paramount contract star who starred in many important silent movies in the 1920s, continuing into the sound era. She is seen with **Johnny Fox** on the cover of a song promoting the legendary silent production *The Covered Wagon*, based on a popular serial story that had been appearing in the *Saturday Evening Post*. (1923)

Eyes of Youth
In *Eyes of Youth* **Clara Kimball Young** portrayed a heroine trying to choose among many suitors, one of whom was a young unknown actor named Rudolph Valentino. She appears here on the cover of the Irving Berlin title song. Other movies from the 1920s include *The Worldly Madonna* and *Lying Wives*. (1919)

Left:
I'd Give Heaven and Earth for You
Clara Kimball Young (1890-1960) began her film career with Vitagraph in 1909 playing pretty ingénues, later moving into serious matronly roles. Some of her memorable parts were Anne Boleyn in *Cardinal Wolsey* (1912), *Camille* (title role, 1915), and *Trilby* (title role, 1915). Her mature good looks and innate dignity are evident on this song cover when she was twenty-six years old. She was at the top of the heap when voted the most popular screen star by fans in 1914, but her career slumped through mismanagement in the early 1920s. (1916)

Opposite Page:
Poor Pauline
Pearl White (1889-1938) became known as the Queen of the Serials, most famous for her portrayal of Pauline, the death-defying heroine of the popular cliff-hanger *The Perils of Pauline* told in 20 episodes. She is seen here on the cover of the serial's theme song that describes in priceless prose the terrible plight of the hapless heroine who delighted and terrified audiences episode after episode. (1914)

POOR PAULINE
MISS PEARL WHITE
STAR OF THE FAMOUS SERIAL PHOTOPLAY
"THE PERILS OF PAULINE"
WORDS BY
CHAS. McCARRON
MUSIC BY
RAYMOND WALKER
BROADWAY MUSIC CORPORATION
WILL VON TILZER PRESIDENT
145 WEST 45th ST NEW YORK
FLOYD N.Y.

CHAPTER 8:
SERIAL PHOTOPLAYS

From about 1914 to 1930 silent movie audiences were entertained with installment serials—thrill-packed adventure stories told in periodic chapters. These suspenseful weekly serials ensured continuing attendance by theatergoers who needed to know if the hero or heroine survived the terrifying episodes from week to week. The idea was to end every installment with a situation so hopeless that nothing could keep the audience from returning to the theater the following week to see how it all turned out. In fact, the word "cliff-hanger" came into use during the silent serial era to describe the impossible plight of a movie character hanging by his or her fingernails from a steep cliff with no relief in sight at the close of an episode—a situation used so often as to become a cliché, but a comfortably predictable cliché. The audience, though on the edge of their seats, knew things would turn out all right, and the dauntless hero or heroine would survive to battle evil deeds another week. Serial devotees enjoyed the convoluted plots and complications, the speedy chases, the last-minute rescues, and especially loved to hiss and boo the villain and cheer the good guys.

Most of the leading stars of these serials are now gone, and many of the films themselves are lost forever, but sheet music survives with photos on the covers of the actors and actresses as they appeared in their heyday providing another historical glance into the silent movie past.

What Happened to Mary, with Mary Fuller in the title role, was the forerunner of the serial. Filmed by the Edison Company in conjunction with a magazine series in McClure's *The Ladies World*, it hit the silent screen in 1912-13 with a new story released monthly. It was actually more of a series than a serial, with a complete story in each feature rather than a continuing episode.

> Excerpt:
> I'm as worried as can be, all the movie shows I see
> Have that awful mystery, Pauline and her perils.
> On a rope they dangle her, then they choke and strangle her,
> With an axe they mangle her, always something new.
>
> Handsome Harry's always near, he will save her never fear.
> Just in time he will appear, when Pauline's in peril.
> On a roof she fights for life, villain sticks her with a knife,
> *'Marry me or be my wife!' what will Pauline do?"*

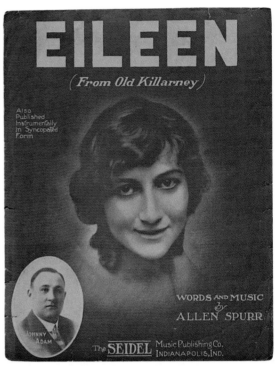

Eileen (from Old Killarney)
Cover star **Mary Fuller** (1893-), a popular leading lady with the Edison Company, played the title role in *What Happened to Mary*, the forerunner of the movie serial, told in 12 chapters. She portrayed a young woman trying to escape the greedy clutches of a wicked foster father who is trying to marry her off against her will. She subsequently made other serials—*Who Will Marry Mary?* (1913—6 chapters), and *The Active Life of Dolly of the Dailies* (1914—12 chapters). Mary Fuller was a plucky little performer who always did her own stunts, frequently taking dangerous risks. (1914)

The Adventures of Kathlyn, starring Kathlyn Williams, was the first authentic serial, a continuing story shown in episodes that usually ended with an unresolved dire situation that left an anxious audience eager to return for the denouement. It was released in 1914, a chapter at a time each week, continuing for several months.

The Perils of Pauline, starring the redoubtable Pearl White, was the most famous of the serials. It followed *The Adventures of Kathlyn* by a few months, and became the model for those to come. It was a 20-chapter suspenseful melodrama that involved the intrepid heroine in perilous, death-defying situations from which she managed to escape, week after week. Other adventurous heroines that followed the successful *Pauline* were played by silent serial stars Grace Cunard, Helen Holmes, and Ruth Roland, among others, in this genre that became a staple of Saturday afternoon matinees at the movies.

Serials had their own theme songs, just as other silent movies did. Most of them promote the title of the photoplay and have a photograph of the main star. The group of song covers shown here is a good representation of the earliest serials, and is listed chronologically to show the growth of the genre.

Kathlyn Waltz
Following the success of *What Happened to Mary* in 1912-13, **Kathlyn Williams** (1888-1960) was featured in the first authentic cliff-hanger serial, *The Adventures of Kathlyn*. Produced by the Selig Polyscope Company, it ran for 13 installments coordinated with the release of a newspaper serial in the *Chicago Tribune*. The serial idea was a financial success; it kept audiences and readers coming back, and the *Tribune* had a 10% increase in circulation. The story told of the adventures of an American girl who inherited a throne in exotic India and the subsequent complications that included such terrors as wild animals on the loose. Miss Williams continued in films until 1935. (1914)

Lucille Love
Universal brought forth a new team of serial stars, **Grace Cunard** (1894-1967) and **Francis Ford** (1882-1953), starring in a string of 15 episodes of *Lucille Love, Girl of Mystery*. They were actively involved in all areas of picture-making—writing, directing, acting, cutting, and title writing—and the finished product was a fine suspenseful serial that made stars of them both. The melodramatic plot dealt with a love triangle and the subsequent lust for revenge by the man who lost the girl, with attendant danger and lump-in-the-throat action scenes. Theme song was dedicated to lovely Grace Cunard who appears on the cover. (1914) *Collection of James Nelson Brown*

Pauline Waltz
Pearl White, one of the most popular stars of her day, made her fame and fortune primarily in serial photoplays. Mystery, suspense, and action were the ingredients, and Miss White usually performed her own stunts that frequently got her into trouble. Tales abound of her exploits when situations went awry—like the time she was carried away in a runaway balloon that wasn't tied down, and fortunately had the presence of mind to release the gas so the balloon could land. In another segment she almost drowned in a flooded mill as the water level neared the ceiling and the hero who was supposed to rescue her almost arrived too late. Another escapade had her diving off a yacht into Florida waters to escape the villain, not knowing the sea was alive with a school of sharks. (1914)

173

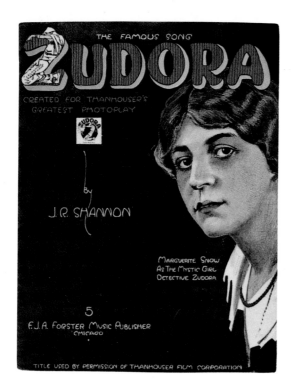

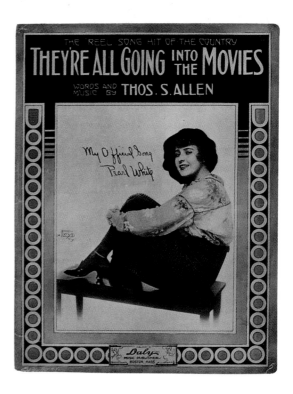

Zudora
Marguerite Snow (1889-1958) played "the mystic girl detective Zudora" in the Thanhouser serial *Zudora (The Twenty Million Dollar Mystery)*, a sequel to an earlier successful serial, *The Million Dollar Mystery*. Her future husband **James Cruze** (1884-1942) co-starred in the 20 episodes playing two roles, a Hindu mystic in heavy makeup and a newspaper reporter. Miss Snow was a beautiful leading lady in other silent movies besides serials from 1911 to 1925, including George M. Cohan's co-star in his first movie *Broadway Jones* in 1917. Miss Snow's second husband was silent screen idol Francis X. Bushman. (1914)

They're All Going into the Movies
Pearl White poses provocatively on the cover of this song by Thomas Allen with lyrics praising the movies, "...The great William Shakespeare wrote many a play but now very seldom they're seen, For maybe you've guessed they have more interest in the perils of Pretty Pauline." (1915)

Elaine, My Moving Picture Queen
In 1914 **Pearl White** introduced the heroine Elaine Dodge in *The Exploits of Elaine*. The fourteen episodes of the serial were so successful that two sequels were made in 1915—*The New Exploits of Elaine* (10 episodes) and *The Romance of Elaine* (12 episodes), for a total of 36 chapters starring the same character. The intrepid heroine in these yarns was an adventurous young lady who was searching for her father's murderer, a mysterious character known as the "Clutching Hand." A large attractive portrait of Pearl White with a facsimile autograph appears on the cover of this movie theme song. "That Clutching Hand" is another song from the serial. (1915)

Left:

Runaway June

Norma Phillips was a stage and screen actress who played the title role in the silent serial *Runaway June* produced by Reliance Motion Picture Company. The plot revolved around the adventures of a young bride who left her husband on their wedding trip and got into all kinds of trouble. It ran for 15 episodes, and was praised for its authenticity with some episodes actually shot on board a steamer in Bermuda. Sheet music of the title theme song shows Miss Phillips with a collie dog. (1915)

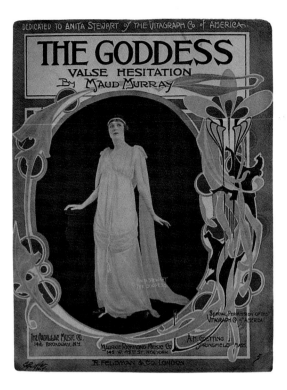

The Goddess

Through 15 episodes of increasing complications, **Anita Stewart** portrayed Celestia, a girl raised by three millionaires to believe she possessed extraordinary heaven-sent power to reform the world. *The Goddess* was praised for its good acting and skillful photography. This promotional song by Maud Murray was dedicated to the beautiful Miss Stewart. (1915)

Like a Diamond from the Sky

Lottie Pickford (1895-1936) starred in the serial *A Diamond From the Sky*, a 30 episode saga produced by American Film Company and directed by William Desmond Taylor. The leading role of Esther was first offered to Mary Pickford who declined because of contractual obligations. and her sister Lottie played the part. The scenario by Roy McCardell won a $10,000 prize sponsored by the *Chicago Tribune*, and revolved around possession of a fabled diamond imbedded in a meteorite that came to earth dramatically in a great ball of fire. (1915)

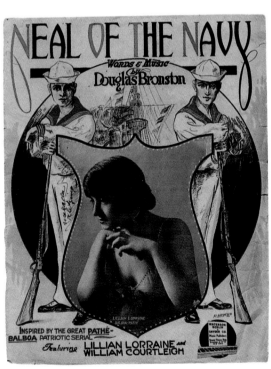

Neal of the Navy

Lillian Lorraine, fabled beauty of the *Ziegfeld Follies*, left the New York stage to play the part of Annette in *Neal of the Navy*, a Pathé-Balboa silent serial with 14 episodes. Despite a plot involving a map, lost treasure, and handsome leading man William Courtleigh, Jr. as the hero Neal Hardin, the serial was not a success. Miss Lorraine appears on the cover of the theme song illustrated by artist Al Barbelle. (1915)

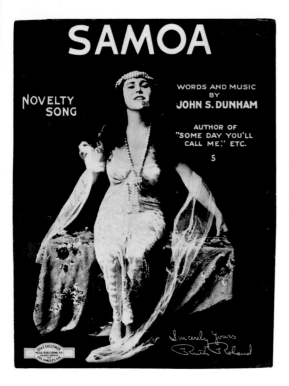

Left:
Samoa
Ruth Roland (1892-1937) was another major star of the silent serials, rivaling Pearl White in popularity and output. In the tradition of Mary Fuller, both she and Pearl prided themselves on doing their own stunts, keeping audiences enthralled with their athletic prowess. When Miss Roland posed for this alluring cover photo she was riding the crest of success with her first Pathé silent serial *The Red Circle*. (1916)

Gloria's Romance
Billie Burke (1885-1970) obtained special permission from husband Florenz Ziegfeld to play the lead in the Kleine production of the silent serial *Gloria's Romance*. No expense was spared in the mounting of the series that ran for 20 episodes, but it flopped despite its lavishness. (1916)

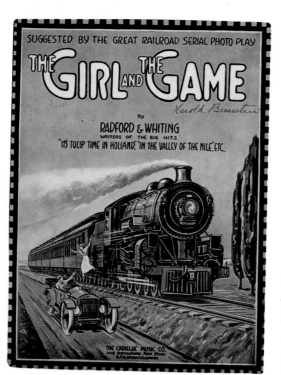

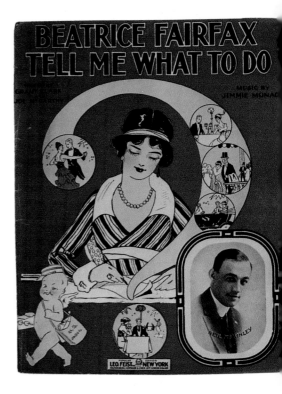

Right:
Beatrice Fairfax
Harry Fox and **Grace Darling** co-starred in 15 episodes of the silent serial *Beatrice Fairfax*, a release by International Film Service. Not much is known of the plot, but provocative chapter titles such as *Adventures of the Jealous Wife*, *The Wages of Sin*, and *The Hidden Menace* titillate the curiosity. The name Beatrice Fairfax is better known as a columnist who answered letters and gave advice to the lovelorn. (1915)

The Girl and The Game
Helen Holmes (1892-1950) was a leading lady in silent serials, many of which had a railroad background. She was a strong athlete and performed her own stunts often atop a moving train with dangerous leaps from train to horse or automobile. She starred in *The Girl and the Game*, a 15 episode serial produced by Signal Film Corporation with her husband J. P. McGowan who also directed the series. (1916)

Right:

The Voice on the Wire

Neva Gerber and **Ben Wilson**, a famous serial team, appeared together for the first time in the exciting 15 episode Universal serial *The Voice on the Wire*. This serial was praised for its fast pace and strong plot involving a chilling mystery voice on the telephone, a secret society who discovered a mummifying technique known as "The Living Death," a sympathetic love story, and much action and violence. The two co-stars are shown on the cover of the theme song. (1917)

The Girl in the Purple Mask

Grace Cunard and **Francis Ford** co-starred in 16 episodes of Universal's silent serial *The Purple Mask*, and appear in a dramatic pose on the cover of the theme song. The convoluted plot starred Miss Cunard as Patricia Montez who became a daring jewel thief named "Queen of the Apaches," and left a purple mask after each robbery. As in other Cunard/Ford serials, the entire production was laced with lively action scenes of fights, narrow escapes, and dangerous stunts. Francis Ford was the older brother of John Ford, and gave John his first opportunity in films. (1917)

Left:

Patria

Irene Castle (1893-1969) was a world acclaimed dancer with her husband and partner Vernon. She played the role of heroine Patria Channing in the 15 episode silent serial *Patria* released by International Film Service and co-starring Warner Oland and Milton Sills. The production bore the heavy hand of William Randolph Hearst who slanted the imaginary story line to stir up enmity against Japan and Mexico, and foster belligerent pro-war feelings. (1917)

The Fatal Ring

The Fatal Ring was a 20 episode serial co-starring **Pearl White** with Earle Fox and Warner Oland. In this taut suspenseful drama, she portrayed Pearl Standish, a rich girl who owns a valuable violet diamond that is being sought by the High Priestess of the Sacred Order of the Violet God, who wants the diamond at any cost. Hair-raising escapades plunge Pearl into dangerous situations in such chapters as *The Crushing Wall, Rays of Death, The Perilous Plunge, The Dagger Duel,* and *The Cryptic Maze.* (1917) *Collection of James Nelson Brown*

Some Day I'll Make You Glad

WORDS BY
Max C. Freedman

MUSIC BY
Harry D. Squires

Ruth Roland

Joe Morris Music Co.
145 WEST 45th ST.
NEW YORK

Left:
Some Day I'll Make You Glad
Ruth Roland started out in vaudeville as "Baby Ruth" when only two years old, and entered films in 1911 for the Kalem Company where she had lots of experience in westerns, melodramas, and comedies. She later went to work for Pathé and starred in many episodic serials including *Who Pays?*, *The Neglected Wife*, *Hands Up!*, *The Tiger's Trail*, *The Avenging Arrow*, *The Timber Queen*, *White Eagle*, *Haunted Valley*, and the Ruth serials culminating in *Ruth of the Range* in 1923. (1918)

ROMANTIC RUTH

THIS SONG INSPIRED BY
THE PATHE SERIAL
"THE ADVENTURES OF RUTH"
STARRING RUTH ROLAND

WORDS BY
ANNELU BURNS

MUSIC BY
MADELYN SHEPPARD

Romantic Ruth
In *The Adventures of Ruth*, **Ruth Roland** portrayed Ruth Robin, the daughter of a millionaire who is shot by a criminal gang known as the "Terrible Thirteen." On his deathbed he implored her to recover the Peacock Fan that contained a secret that affected her, and told her she would receive thirteen separate keys, each one vital to her solving the mystery of the fan. The plot took 15 episodes to unravel including cliff-hanging climaxes involving the brave and dauntless heroine. Miss Roland appears on the cover of the theme song from the movie serial, her image superimposed on one of the mysterious keys. (1920)

Why do they call Mama Poor Butterfly

WORDS BY
LOUIS SEIFERT

MUSIC BY
W. C. POLLA

C. C. CHURCH AND COMPANY, HARTFORD, CONN., U.S.A.

Why Do They Call Mama Poor Butterfly
Ruth Roland was beautiful as well as talented. At age sixteen while playing ingénue roles on the stage, she was noticed by the famous New York artist, Harrison Fisher, who asked her to pose for him. Ten years later as a major silent film star she posed for this lithograph cover drawing by artist Emmett O. Smith for the Knapp Company. (1919)

Right:
The Evil Eye
Cover star **Benny Leonard** came to the movies from the world of prize-fighting where he held the lightweight boxing championship from 1917-1925. He made the 15-chapter serial *The Evil Eye* for Hallmark Pictures, co-starring with veteran actor Stuart Holmes. Leonard made another movie with Hoot Gibson in 1928, *Flying Fists*, in which he donned the gloves on screen. This theme song was written by Mr. Leonard with Alex Sullivan and Jack Mills. (1920) *Collection of Harold Jacobs*

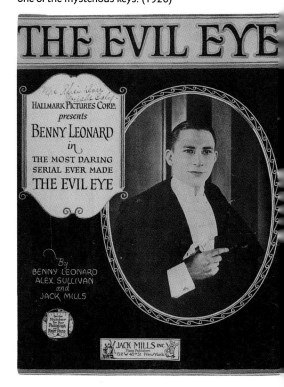

THE EVIL EYE

HALLMARK PICTURES CORP.
presents
BENNY LEONARD
in
THE MOST DARING
SERIAL EVER MADE
THE EVIL EYE

By
BENNY LEONARD
ALEX. SULLIVAN
and
JACK MILLS

JACK MILLS INC.

The Santa Fe Trail
Tiny **Neva Gerber**, a Chicago society girl before she entered films, was touted as a top-notch actress. She co-starred with Jack Perrin in *The Santa Fe Trail*, a 15 episode historical serial filmed by the Arrow company. (1923)

Love Thoughts of You
Jacqueline Logan and **Walter Miller** starred in *King of the Kongo*, a Mascot Pictures serial that was released in two versions—silent and sound. This taut serial had all the ingredients for a top-notch thriller including a Secret Service agent and a beautiful girl in a remote jungle searching for buried treasure, a ferocious gorilla, a deadly lion's pit, and even an appearance by Boris Karloff. Lee Zahler composed a special synchronized musical score for the serial, and also wrote the music for this theme song. (1929) *Collection of Harold Jacob*

☆ ☆ ☆ ☆ ☆

Motion pictures were an established art form in the late 1920s, but sound was making inroads into the medium. Music accompaniment was always considered an important adjunct to the action on the screen but when a sound track with dialogue was added, the death knell rang for the old way of making movies.

The Jazz Singer starring Al Jolson opened in October of 1927, and it made movie history. Though much of it was silent, it included some great Jolson songs and a few speaking lines. It created a sensation with the movie-going public and made over two million dollars for Warner Brothers. Sound movies soon became top priority, and movie studios hastened to adapt to the demand.

During the transition period to sound, silent movies that were in production had sound effects and music added, and by the end of 1929 the silent movie was virtually a thing of the past.

In resurrecting and preserving sheet music from the silent movie era, we hope to show our appreciation to the early motion picture pioneers—the producers, directors, cameramen, stuntmen, and most of all, to the players.

BIBLIOGRAPHY

Bergan, Ronald. *The United Artists Story*. New York: Crown Publishers, Inc., 1986.

Brownlow, Kevin. *The Parade's Gone By*. Berkeley: University of California Press, 1968.

Chaplin, Charles. *My Autobiography*. London: The Bodley Head, 1964.

Cooper, Miriam, with Bonnie Herndon. *Dark Lady of the Silents*. Indianapolis and New York: The Bobbs-Merrill Company, 1973.

Eames, John Douglas. *The MGM Story*. N. Y.: Crescent Books, 1987.

_____.*The Paramount Story*. New York: Crown Publishers, 1987.

Engel, Lehman. *The American Musical Theater*. New York: A CBS Legacy Collection Book, 1967.

Everson, William K. *American Silent Film*. New York: Oxford University Press, 1978.

Farnsworth, Marjorie. *The Ziegfeld Follies*. New York: Bonanza Books, 1956.

Fernett, Gene. *Poverty Row*. Florida: Coral Reef Publication, Inc., 1973.

Franklin, Joe. *Classics of the Silent Screen*. New York: Cadillac Publishing Company, Inc., 1959.

Gammond, Peter. *The Oxford Companion to Popular Music*. New York: Oxford University Press, 1993.

Geduld, Harry M. *The Birth of the Talkies*. Indiana University Press, 1975.

Gill, Brendan, Edited by Robert Kimball. *Cole*. New York: Holt Rinehart & Winston, 1972.

Green, Stanley. *Encyclopedia of the Musical Theatre*. New York: Dodd, Mead & Company, 1976.

_____. *The World of Musical Comedy*. New York: Da Capo Press Inc.,1988.

Heide, Robert, and John Gilman. *Starstruck, the Wonderful World of Movie Memorabilia*. New York: Doubleday and Company, 1986.

Henderson, Robert M. *D. W. Griffith, His Life and Work*. New York: Oxford University Press, *1972*.

Hirschhorn, Clive. *The Universal Story*. New York: Crown Publishers, 1983.

_____. *The Warner Brothers Story*. New York: Crown Publishers, 1986.

Jacobs, Dick and Harriet. *Who Wrote That Song?* Cinncinnati, Ohio: Writer's Digest Books, 1994.

Jewell, Richard B., with Vernon Harbin. *The RKO Story*. New York: Arlington House, 1982.

Katz, Ephraim. *The Film Encyclopedia*. New York: Perigee Books, 1979.

Kimball, Robert, and Alfred Simon. *The Gershwins*. New York: Atheneum, 1973.

Kirkpatrick, Sidney D. *A Cast of Killers*. New York: E. P. Dutton, 1986.

Lahue, Kalton C. *Continued Next Week, A History of the Moving Picture Serial*. University of Oklahoma Press, 1964.

_____.*Gentlemen to the Rescue*. New York: Castle Books, 1972.

Laufe, Abe. *Broadway's Greatest Musicals*. New York: Funk & Wagnalls, 1977.

Mordden, Ethan. *Better Foot Forward*. New York: Grossman Publishers, 1976.

Rapée, Erno. *Motion Picture Moods*. New York: G. Schirmer, 1924.

Scott, Evelyn F. *Hollywood When Silents Were Golden*. New York: McGraw-Hill Book Company, 1972.

Slide, Anthony. *Silent Portraits*. New York: The Vestal Press, Ltd., 1989.

Smith, Cecil. *Musical Comedy in America*. New York: Theatre Arts Books: Robert M. MacGregor, 1950.

Spaeth, Sigmund. *A History of Popular Music in America*. New York: Random House, 1948.

Spears, Jack. *Hollywood: The Golden Era*. New Jersey: A. S. Barnes and Co., 1971.

Stewart, John. *Filmarama, Vol.II. The Flaming Years, 1920-1929*. New Jersey, The Scarecrow Press, Inc., 1977.

Stubblebine, Donald J. *Cinema Sheet Music*. North Carolina: McFarland & Company, Inc., 1991.

Suskin, Steven. *Show Tunes 1905-1985*. New York: Dodd, Mead & Company, 1986.

Taylor, Deems. *A Pictorial History of the Movies*. New York: Simon and Schuster, Inc., 1943.

Wagenknecht, Edward. *The Movies in the Age of Innocence*. New York: Ballantine Books, 1971.

Wiley, Mason, and Damien Bona. *Inside Oscar*. New York: Ballantine Books, 1988.

Ziegfeld, Richard, and Paulette Ziegfeld. *The Ziegfeld Touch*. New York: Harry N. Abrams, Inc., 1993.

Television Series: "Hollywood." Written, directed, and produced by Kevin Brownlow and David Gill. A Thames Colour Production.

SONG INDEX AND VALUE GUIDE

Broadway show and silent movie music are more in demand than most common garden variety songs that are encountered at garage sales, flea markets, and antique stores, and prices start at around two dollars minimum. Prices escalate dramatically for rarer pieces from pre-1900 shows, and for songs with covers of coveted silent movie stars such as Lillian Gish, Clara Bow, Rudolph Valentino, Charlie Chaplin, and for songs from D. W. Griffith movies.

Many variables enter into pricing—rarity, demand, historical significance of the movie or show, cover personality, and condition. The following value guide is based on a combination of dealers' set price lists, published price guides, auction sales, and the author's own experience. Prices in *italics* are documented prices known to have been paid at dealers' auctions, which are extremely variable and unpredictable. One can get lucky and pick up a rare piece below market value if the high bidders already have it.

The stated price is for illustrated pieces in *excellent* condition, and should be discounted for lower grades as described in the following condition chart.

Excellent—Very clean, paper still crisp, virtually flawless. May have a music store stamp or a price sticker, as old music store stock was routinely price-stickered in the 1960s and '70s. Full value.

Good—Piece in nice shape, desirable for a collection with no immediate need to upgrade. May show some wear—small tears (less than 3/4"), careful taped repair on inside, inconspicuous signature, store stamp, or price sticker on cover. 25% discount.

Fair—Considerable wear from use, and one or more problems like light soil, creases, tears, frayed edges, separated cover, prominent signatures, stickers, or name stamps. 50% discount.

Poor—Complete, but with one or more mutilation problems, such as ragged edges with large tears or pieces missing, folds and/or creases, heavy soiling, sloppy taped repairs, bold writing or doodling, trimmed down from large size. Generally too worn to be of collectible value, unless rare and in a major collectible category. 90% discount.

SHOW AND MOVIE INDEX

(Note: Use to locate illustrated songs. Shows are in italics.)

SILENT FILM STAR INDEX